"Thanks to Professor Hae-Seok, Yoo's meticulous research in Robert Jermain Thomas's native Wales, the Korean Church can now encounter the man behind the myth: Thomas, not merely a hero or distant figure, but a life of profound significance and reverence. At a time when the Korean Church longs for revival, this book allows us to see mission through Thomas's eyes and heart. It reminds today's Christians of their responsibilities, offering lessons of courage, faith, and dedication. This work stands as both a guide to renewed revival and a compass for thoughtful, mature mission. I wholeheartedly recommend it."

—DANIEL LEE

Founding and Senior Pastor Emeritus, Global Mission Church

"*The First Protestant Martyr in Korea from Wales* presents a carefully researched and well-grounded account of early Protestant martyrdom in Korea. Drawing on previously unused sources from Thomas's Welsh homeland, Hae-Seok, Yoo traces the historical and ecclesial connections between Welsh Protestantism and emerging Korean Christianity. This study offers a concise yet meaningful contribution to both Korean and global church history."

—YOUNG MIN KIM

Adjunct Professor of Missiology, Chongshin University

"The Korean church has achieved extraordinary growth within Christianity's two-thousand-year history. Many scholars seek the origins of this spiritual flourishing. Echoing Tertullian's maxim, 'The church is founded upon the blood of martyrs,' the Korean church stands upon the sacrifice of Robert J. Thomas. Commemorating his 160th anniversary, we proudly present his legacy globally. This monograph—reflecting Dr. Hae-Seok, Yoo's extensive research—provides critical insights for those investigating the foundations of Korean Christianity."

—SUNGKYU PARK

President, Chongshin University

"In *The First Protestant Martyr in Korea from Wales*, Professor Yoo invites us to read Thomas's martyrdom not merely as history but as a living call to North Korea mission today. The blood shed by the Taedong River became a seed of the gospel, and its debt still rests upon the Korean church. Grounded in careful scholarship, this book testifies that God will ultimately open a path for the gospel to the closed land."

—KWANG MIN HA

Director Professor, Graduate School of Korean Unification and Development, Chongshin University

The First Protestant Martyr in Korea from Wales

The First Protestant Martyr in Korea from Wales

The Life and Ministry of Robert Jermain Thomas

HAE-SEOK, YOO

WIPF & STOCK · Eugene, Oregon

THE FIRST PROTESTANT MARTYR IN KOREA FROM WALES
The Life and Ministry of Robert Jermain Thomas

Copyright © 2026 Hae-Seok, Yoo. All rights reserved. Except for brief quotations in critical publications or reviews, no part of this book may be reproduced in any manner without prior written permission from the publisher. Write: Permissions, Wipf and Stock Publishers, 199 W. 8th Ave., Suite 3, Eugene, OR 97401.

Wipf & Stock
An Imprint of Wipf and Stock Publishers
199 W. 8th Ave., Suite 3
Eugene, OR 97401

www.wipfandstock.com

PAPERBACK ISBN: 979-8-3852-6754-5
HARDCOVER ISBN: 979-8-3852-6755-2
EBOOK ISBN: 979-8-3852-6756-9

VERSION NUMBER 011226

Scripture quotations are taken from The Holy Bible, New International Version®, NIV®. Copyright © 1973, 1978, 1984, 2011 by Biblica, Inc. Used with permission of Zondervan. All rights reserved worldwide. www.zondervan.com.

I would like to record my sincere appreciation for my wife, Han Hyun-Ju, whose steadfast companionship over the past thirty-three years—across Egypt, Wales, and Korea—has been an enduring source of support throughout the course of my life and ministry.

I am likewise grateful to my two sons, Ju Hyung in Bristol and Ye Hyoung in London, whose growth and maturity continue to be a source of pride. I extend to them my warm affection and heartfelt thanks.

Contents

Prologue | ix
Introduction | xi

CHAPTER 1
Thomas in Wales, Britain | 1

CHAPTER 2
Thomas in Shanghai, China | 18

CHAPTER 3
Settling and New Opportunities in Chefoo | 35

CHAPTER 4
The First Visit to Korea | 47

CHAPTER 5
Peking: A Season of Mission Integration | 66

CHAPTER 6
The Second Visit to Korea | 80

CHAPTER 7
The Martyrdom of Thomas and His Missionary Legacy | 112

Bibliography | 135

Prologue

THE KOREAN CHURCH HAD experienced growth and revival at a pace nearly unprecedented in global Christian history. Missionaries laid the foundation through education, healthcare, and Bible translation. Through strong cooperation among denominations, systematic training, and passionate sending, the Korean church rapidly became one of the world's leading missionary-sending nations—transitioning from a mission field to a mission force in just decades. As Samuel A. Moffett, who served in Pyongyang, observed that Korean Christianity truly began with Robert Jermain Thomas, the first to carry the Gospel into inland Korea. Though his ministry was brief, its impact remains unmatched in the history of Christian mission.

Few missionaries in Korean history have been as widely misunderstood as Robert Jermain Thomas. In the early Korean church, his death was celebrated as heroic, and for decades, he was honored as Joseon's first great Protestant martyr. During Japan's colonial rule, however, the *General Sherman* incident was reframed as an American attempt to invade Korea, and Thomas was branded an enemy of the Korean people. North Korea later transformed this distortion into national myth, claiming that Kim Ŭngu (Kim Il Sung's great-grandfather) led the attack on the *General Sherman* and that Kim Bo-hyon (Kim Il Sung's grandfather) personally killed Thomas. To this day, North Koreans are taught that Thomas was an American spy, not a British missionary. Debate over his martyrdom and legacy continues.

Although Thomas's impact on the Korean church was profound, research into his life remains incomplete. Much of the controversy stems from the scarcity of reliable sources and the enduring power of myth over documented fact.

Since 1990, I had undergone missionary training in Wales and had served as a missionary in Egypt. Starting in 1997, I became the president of

Prologue

a mission organization there while also supporting the churches in the UK under the Presbyterian Church of Wales.

As the year 2000 approached, I was moved by the legacy of Robert Jermain Thomas and gratitude for how the Welsh church had sent him to Korea as a missionary. To express thanks, I invited church leaders from across Wales and hosted a special gathering at St. David's Hall in Cardiff. This event was featured as top news by BBC1, BBC2, ITV, and S4C. Shortly after, Stephen Rees—the fifth-generation descendant of Thomas's sister—came to see me and presented me with a pink cloth bundle, which contained Thomas's letters to his parents and many letters he had exchanged with Elder Oh Moon-hwan, who published a book about Thomas in 1927.

Two decades ago, I published *Thomas Moksa-jeon* (The Story of Robert Jermain Thomas), which became a bestseller. Later, I earned a master of philosophy (MPhil) degree from the University of Wales through research on Thomas. Thereafter, I received my Doctor of Theology (Th.D) degree from the Graduate School of Calvin University. Currently, I serve as a professor, Dean of Graduate School of Intercultural Studies at Chongshin University, teaching and mentoring future leaders. As the one hundred sixtieth anniversary of Thomas's martyrdom approaches, I have taken up my pen once again to compile and present a scholarly account of Thomas's life. While *Thomas Moksa-jeon* focused on storytelling, this work aims to provide a theoretical and academic exploration of Thomas's legacy.

This work adopts a distinctly academic approach, tracing Thomas's journey from his early education in Wales, through his formative years with the LMS and his pioneering settlement in China, to his fateful mission in Korea. Drawing extensively on previously unused primary sources, I address long-standing controversies about Thomas's final days and martyrdom, offering balanced and authoritative explanations. The book critically assesses existing interpretations—many shaped by the political agendas of the US, Japan, China, and North Korea—and seeks to clarify Thomas's true significance as the first Protestant missionary and martyr in Korean church history.

By empirically investigating Thomas's motivations, missionary strategies, and the historical context of his death, this work aims to correct persistent misunderstandings and highlight the enduring missiological and theological importance of his legacy for Korean Christianity—and for the global church.

Introduction

THE YEAR 2026 MARKS the 160th anniversary of the martyrdom of Robert Jermain Thomas (1839–1866), a missionary from Wales who died on the banks of the Daedong River in Korea in 1866. Over the years, how people interpreted Thomas's sacrifice shifted with Korea's turbulent modern history. Yet, the early Korean Protestant community consistently viewed his death as a genuine martyrdom and remembered it with deep respect.

In August 1909, a commemorative ceremony in Pyongyang, marking twenty-five years of Protestant mission in Korea honored that legacy. American missionary Samuel A. Moffett looked back on those early years and boldly stated that Korean Christianity truly began with Robert Jermain Thomas, who entered Joseon[1] in 1865 to proclaim the gospel. Moffett emphasized that Thomas had boldly distributed New Testaments and personally connected with individuals who had received them—underscoring Thomas's pivotal role in igniting the Korean missionary movement:

> The first Protestant Missionary to enter Korea was a Scotch Presbyterian; the Rev. Mr. Thomas who, in 1865, as a colporteur of the Scotch Bible Society, from a Chinese junk scattered Chinese Scriptures along the coast of Whang Hai province, and in 1866, when connected with the London Missionary Society, came to Pyeng Yang on the "*General Sherman*" bringing with him Chinese Scriptures. He perished with the crew of that vessel being cut to pieces and burned on the bank of the river just below the city, but not until he had given out the copies of the New Testament which he had. The writer has met some of those who received these

---

1. In this book, the dynasty of Korea from 1392 to 1910 is referred to as "Joseon" in accordance with the modern Revised Romanization standards (the current official Korean romanization system). However, when referencing historic book titles or works originally published under the McCune-Reischauer romanization—an older system for transcribing Korean—we preserve the original spelling using "Choseon."

Introduction

books and among the early catechumens received was one whose father had for years one of these books in his house. It was in 1866 that the "*General Sherman*" and her crew perished, the only now known relic here being the chains binding the pillars in the pavilion above the East Gate.[2]

In September 1912, during the annual meeting of the American Presbyterian Mission in Korea held in Seoul, a special Thomas Memorial Committee was appointed to honor Robert Jermain Thomas's contributions. The committee included Samuel A. Moffett (1852–1939), Frederick S. Miller (1886–1932), and George S. McCune (1872–1941).[3] On September 11, 1926, the fifteenth General Assembly of the Presbyterian Church in Korea marked the sixtieth anniversary of Thomas's martyrdom with a gathering held in Pyongyang—the very city where he died. The following year, in 1927, the Thomas Memorial Association was officially established with Samuel Moffett serving as its president and Oh Mun-hwan appointed as its secretary-general. That same year also marked the thirtieth anniversary of the founding of the Korean branch of the British and Foreign Bible Society. To celebrate both occasions, a special memorial service took place at Seungdong Church in Seoul. Dr. Won Han-kyung (son of Horace Underwood) and Pastor Seo Kyung-jo led the worship service.[4]

The 1928 publication *Joseon Yesugyo Changnohoe Sagi* (A History of the Presbyterian Church of Joseon) begins its preface with the following words:

> Joseon, a nation in the East, had long kept its doors closed to the outside world. The people sought to protect themselves from foreign influence, content to remain a hermit kingdom. This strong resistance to Western contact included a reluctance to embrace Christianity, which prevented them from receiving the gift of eternal life. Yet, in His boundless mercy, God so loved the people of Joseon that He sent them a devoted servant, only for that servant to meet a martyr's death. That man was none other than Reverend Robert Jermain Thomas.[5]

In 1931, Japan seized control of Manchuria. By 1937, they had launched a full-scale invasion of China—the Second Sino-Japanese

---

2. Moffett, "Evangelistic Work," 14.
3. Baek, *Han'guk Gaesin Kyohoe-sa 1832–1910*, 42
4. Oh, *Thomas Moksa-jeon*, appendix, 6.
5. Cha, *Joseon Yesugyo Jangrogyohoe Sagi*, 11.

INTRODUCTION

War—and, within two years, occupied ten Chinese provinces. Japan later used these conquests to justify its expansion into the Pacific. As part of this effort, Japanese propaganda revived the *General Sherman* incident, twisting it into a story of an attempted American invasion of Joseon (Korea). In this rewritten narrative, Reverend Robert Jermain Thomas—a man who had come solely to evangelize—was recast as an enemy of the Korean people.

> When the Second Sino-Japanese War began in 1937, the Japanese government moved quickly to assert control. By early 1939, they had issued a complete ban on all commemorative events held by foreign missionaries in Korea—effectively halting gospel outreach. One church, long named in honor of Thomas, was forced to take the village's name, Jowang-ri, erasing his legacy from its identity. Even more tragically, the inscription on a monument sent by the directors of the Scottish Bible Society—Thomas's own sending agency—was removed. With the outbreak of the Pacific War (known in Japan as the Greater East Asia War), Japanese propaganda recast Reverend Robert Jermain Thomas—a gospel pioneer and the first Protestant missionary martyr in Korea—as a vanguard of Western invasion, twisting his memory into a tool for manipulation. At the same time, persecution against the Christian community intensified across Korea.[6]

By 1939, the Japanese Government-General of Chosen had expelled all foreign missionaries from Korea and banned any commemorations of their work. The Thomas Memorial Church, for example, was forced to take the name of its village, becoming Jowang-ri Church, while the monument erected by the Scottish Bible Society was concealed under a layer of cement. As the Pacific War began in December 1941, Japanese authorities staged propaganda plays, such as "Daedong River" and "Nakrang" (Lelang), portraying Thomas's arrival as the spearhead of an American imperialist invasion.[7] Under these circumstances, Thomas's life remained buried under official distortion until Korea's liberation from Japan in 1945. Meanwhile, North Korea's *Chosŏn Chŏnsa* (Complete History of Joseon) not only describes the *General Sherman* incident as the first attack on Korea by "the imperialist capitalist state, America," but also misidentifies Missionary Thomas as an American.

---

6. Oh, *Thomas moksa soonkyo*, 9–10.
7. Oak Sung-deuk, "1866 Pyeongyangyangnan kwa Thomas ui Sunkyo," 194.

Introduction

> Despite heavy gunfire and shelling from the enemy (the American ship General Sherman), a suicide squad launched a final fire attack at noon. The commander of this unit was Kim Ung-u, the great-grandfather of Kim Il Sung. He ordered small boats—laden with dry wood and sprinkled with sulfur—to be set adrift down the river toward the grounded and burning General Sherman. Eventually, the enemy abandoned the fight as their ship burned and was on the verge of sinking. The vessel's powder magazine then exploded with a tremendous roar, and black smoke engulfed the skies over Pyongyang. Of the 24 crew members, 13 were incinerated, while the rest jumped into the river and swam to the bank, only to be killed there. Thomas was on the burning ship with his friend. Both he and his friend were killed by the enraged Korean people. The arrogant imperialist American enemies were all killed by the Korean people. This must be understood as judgment delivered by the Korean people.[8]

In their process of idolizing Kim Il Sung, North Korea propagated a myth that his great-grandfather, Kim Ung-u—who was only nine years old at the time—was a fervent fighter who single-handedly defeated the *General Sherman*. Kim Il Sung then politically leveraged this myth to portray his own family as heroic figures. In North Korean history, Thomas was branded an American imperialist spy and was consistently depicted as an American, not a Briton. To this day, North Korea exhibits the USS *Pueblo*, an American spy ship, at the very spot where the *General Sherman* sank, and they maintain a monument commemorating the "victory" over the *General Sherman*.[9]

In the 1980s, although Robert Jermain Thomas continued to be recognized as a missionary in Korea, his legacy was actively reexamined and became a subject of renewed scholarly debate. During this period, academic discourse in South Korea shifted toward studying Christian history from a Korean, recipient-centered perspective. Among those leading this reexamination, Lee Man-yeol notably challenged the notion of Thomas as a martyr. In a 1985 lecture titled "Special Topics in Korean Church History," he argued that there is insufficient historical evidence to support the Korean

---

8. Kwahak Paekkwa Chulpan-sa, *Chosŏn Chŏnsa*, 68–69.

9. Inscription, Monument Commemorating the Defeat of the American Pirate Ship, General Sherman, Hansajong, Pyongyang. The inscription reads, "On September 2, 1866, at Hansajong on the Daedong River, ardent patriot Kim Ung-u and the citizens of Pyongyang victoriously defeated the American pirate ship (the General Sherman)." Quoted in Goh, *Thomaswa hamgea denanun soonrea yeohaeng*, 304.

INTRODUCTION

church's view of Thomas as a martyr—and suggested that the narrative of Thomas's death may be more legend crafted by church leaders than fact.

> While Pastor Thomas was indeed brutally killed, that alone does not elevate him historically to a figure of greatness. The illegal entry of the *General Sherman* into Joseon does not justify viewing his intentions as benign, nor does Thomas's involvement in that incident warrant an inflated assessment of his legacy. Although many churches were later established near the Daedong River—where his blood was shed—directly linking his death to church planting is too simplistic a conclusion. It is time for the Korean church to reevaluate whether Thomas's death truly qualifies as martyrdom.[10]

In the rapidly shifting currents of Korea's modern history, Robert Jermain Thomas's image has taken on layers of religious and political meaning shaped by the times. These shifting interpretations reflect both the scarcity of primary sources about his life and the tendency to focus on the *General Sherman* incident—his arrival in Pyongyang by ship—often leading to politically skewed readings of his life and mission. Thomas's story has, in effect, been appropriated by Koreans to serve various political agendas. Only by adopting a multidimensional and balanced approach can we more fully understand Thomas's legacy. To view him solely through the lens of the *General Sherman*—or any single event—is not only to misunderstand the broader contours of his life but also to ignore the limitations of the surviving historical evidence.

This work approaches Thomas's life in three main ways. First, I seek to uncover what truly motivated him, without distorting the facts of his life. Both the events immediately surrounding the *General Sherman* incident and the broader arc of his time in Korea are interpreted carefully, respecting the best available historical evidence. Second, I explore how his beliefs and actions were shaped by his personality, upbringing, and background. Finally, I examine Thomas's life and ministry within the wider context of his networks, education, and the wider world of the mid-nineteenth century—a turbulent era in both Britain and East Asia.

Thomas's identity as a missionary stands at the heart of this work. I begin by carefully examining his Christian motivations—essential, after all, for someone who gave his life to mission. His strategies and attitudes as a missionary are crucial for understanding the circumstances of his death. Equally important is tracing the impact of the spatial and cultural shifts

---

10. Lee Man-yeol, *Hanguk Kidokgyosa Teukgang*, 36.

Introduction

Thomas experienced, and how these shaped his personal journey. For this reason, I pay special attention to the places where he lived and served: Wales, Britain, Shanghai, Chefoo, Peking, and Korea. At each step, I analyze his actions and decisions in light of his missionary calling. To best understand his motivations and goals, I rely primarily on evidence drawn from key events in his life.

Page numbers and full publication information for some historical sources were not available at the time of this writing. Copies of all birth certificates, marriage licenses, letters, and newspaper articles referenced but not listed in the bibliography are in the author's personal possession.

Chapter 1

Thomas in Wales, Britain

1. HIS FATHER, ROBERT THOMAS

ROBERT JERMAIN THOMAS WAS born in 1839 in Rhayader, Radnorshire, in mid-Wales.[1] His father, Robert Thomas (1809–1884), served as a minister in the Congregational Church. Thomas was raised in the British Congregational Church, which has historically adhered to Calvinist theology and traces its origins to the sixteenth-century English Puritan movement. Especially significant among its independent theologians are John Owen (1616–1683) and Thomas Goodwin (1600–1680), who upheld Reformed doctrines while advocating Congregationalism.[2] In the early nineteenth century, the Congregational Church experienced an evangelical revival that placed greater emphasis on Calvinist soteriology—including the doctrine of predestination. Prominent figures in that revival included William Jay (1769–1853) and Sir Robert Hall (1764–1831), both of whom strongly promoted Reformed theology.[3]

Robert Thomas was born on May 22, 1809, in Rhosllanerchrugog, near Wrexham in northern Wales.[4] From his youth, he attended Bethlehem Chapel, pastored by William Williams (1781–1840). William Williams was a renowned Welsh preacher at the time and, along with Ebenezer Morris

---

1. Certified copy of an entry of birth, no. 153, given June 20, 1985 at the General Register Office, London.

2. Owen, *Death of Death*, 7–10.

3. Jay, *Morning Exercises for the Closet*, 20–22.

4. Robert Thomas, birth certification from Denbighshire Record Office, reference no. 565.

and John Elias, was considered one of the leading figures in the region.[5] Like Timothy being mentored by the apostle Paul, Robert Thomas received spiritual training under William Williams.[6] He took great pride in this mentorship, which continued to influence him throughout his life and was even mentioned during his retirement address:

> Having commenced your religious career, in early youth, under the singularly advantageous auspices of the seraphic William Williams, of Wern, you largely imbibed his genial, wise, and religious spirit, and through the grace of God you have been enabled to retain and constantly manifest it from the outset of your public life to the present day.[7]

Robert Thomas entered a seminary established by the Welsh Congregational Church at the age of eighteen. While studying there, he and his friend Joseph Williams translated Joseph Abbott's *The Mother at Home* into Welsh. The book's reputation grew significantly thanks to a preface by William Williams, which boosted sales and provided financial support to Robert Thomas.[8]

Robert Thomas began his ministry at Shiloh Church in Swansea, South Wales, and was ordained as pastor on April 19, 1837. His mentor, William Williams, traveled all the way from Liverpool—a considerable distance at the time—to attend the ordination service and deliver the sermon. Williams offered three key exhortations to Pastor Thomas: First, a minister draws strength and passion from deep, personal communion with God; therefore, nurturing this relationship is essential. Second, effective preaching stems not from technique but from prayer; a prayerful preacher is a powerful preacher. Third, resisting the adversary's attacks requires prayer and fasting, which serve as the primary means of spiritual defense.[9]

---

5. Evans, *Revival Comes to Wales*, 117.

6. *Adroddiad Jubili Dyled Siloh*, 5.

7. "Robert Thomas Retirement Address," *Abergavenny Chronicle and Monmouthshire Advertiser.*

8. Joseph Abbott's full name was J. S. C. Abbott; the Welsh translation appeared in 1836 (Thomas, *Hanes Eglwysi Annibynnol Cymru*, 15).

9. Mrs. Richards, *Pulpid Siloh, yn cynnwys Atgofion am Hen Weinidogion* [Siloh Pulpit including memories of Siloh's old ministers], an essay read at the church's Cultural Society, Siloh Glandŵr, Oct. 23, 1916.

Thomas in Wales, Britain

After becoming pastor, Robert Thomas married Mary Lloyd Williams (1817–1895) in May 1837.[10] Mary, originally from Newtown, had accompanied him during his three years of study. Together, they shared forty-seven years as life partners. Their first son, Calvin William Thomas, was born in Swansea on February 13, 1838.[11] During Mary's pregnancy with their second child, her health declined due to Swansea's air pollution. Consequently, Robert Thomas resigned from his position at Shiloh Church, where he had served for two years, and moved to Tabernacle Church in Rhayader. Rhayader, a rural town near Mary's hometown of Newtown, offered a healthier environment compared to the industrial city of Swansea. The Tabernacle Church, established in 1688, is one of the oldest Nonconformist chapels in Wales.[12]

There was no parsonage for the minister in Rhayader. However, Reverend Robert Thomas, accustomed to a life of frugality and simplicity, resided in the home of a church member on East Street. It was in this house, on September 7, 1839, that Robert Jermain Thomas—who would later be martyred while proclaiming the gospel in Korea—was born amidst the blessings of the congregation and his family.

> For about two years after this the church remained without a pastor until the Rev. Robert Thomas, Landore, Swansea, was invited, and settled here towards the end of 1839. Just about that time a great revival broke out at the Troedrhiwdalar, and its influence was felt at Rhayader, so much so that in 1841 Mr. Thomas gave the right hand of fellowship to something like a hundred people, while during the other years of his ministry there were also constant additions to the church.[13]

John Thomas, the church historian who visited Robert Thomas's church, said,

> I visited the place towards the end of the revival, and the effects were quite evident. They broke out in the sound of songs and praise, and Mr. Thomas was to them as "the solo song of one in love, singing with melody." Services were held almost entirely in

---

10. *Adroddiad Jubili Dyled Siloh*, 5.

11. Calvin William Thomas, certified copy of an entry of birth given Jan. 26, 2005 at the General Register Office, London; Calvin William Thomas's son, Robert Clifford Lloyd Thomas to Oh Mun-hwan, June 9, 1931, Newport.

12. Jones and Jones, *Brecon and Radnor Congregationalism 1662*, 103.

13. Jones and Jones, *Brecon and Radnor Congregationalism 1662*, 103.

Welsh at that time. Mr. Thomas remained there with great respect until 1848.[14]

In 1847, Reverend Robert Thomas received a call to serve as the pastor of Hanover Church in Monmouthshire, a county situated between England and Wales, and he took up the position the following year.[15] Hanover was divided into Upper and Lower Hanover. Lower Hanover, where the church was located, had about one hundred sixty residents across roughly twenty households. Upper Hanover, a few kilometers away, had a population of approximately two thousand. Soon after his move to Hanover Church, cholera broke out in parts of South Wales in 1849, leading to numerous deaths. As a result, thousands converted to Christianity the following year. According to research by Thomas Rees, 9,139 new believers joined sixty-seven Independent churches within Monmouthshire. Robert Thomas then ministered passionately at Hanover Church for the next thirty-seven years. After retiring from Hanover Church, he stayed in Bristol before moving to his daughter Annie Germaine Stephens's home in Newport. He passed away there on October 12, 1884, at the age of seventy-five.[16]

Robert Thomas was not a revivalist on the scale of Howell Harris, Christmas Evans, or Humphrey Jones. Nevertheless, the churches he led all experienced growth. He was a gentle, gospel-centered Christian gentleman of admirable character. At sixty-two, Robert Thomas inherited a substantial estate from his mother-in-law, yet he donated much of it to public foundations benefiting the poor. He also endowed a £500 scholarship to the seminary from which he graduated, and a scholarship fund bearing his name was established.[17] He took pride in the death of his son, Robert Jermain Thomas, regarding him as "a missionary of outstanding learning and virtue sent by the London Missionary Society." Yet he mourned his son's death deeply.[18]

---

14. Thomas, *Hanes Eglwysi Annibynnol Cymru*, 16.
15. Thomas, *Hanes Eglwysi Annibynnol Cymru*, 35.
16. Evans, *Revival Comes to Wales*.
17. Thomas, *Hanes Eglwysi Annibynnol Cymru*, 16.
18. "Robert Thomas Retirement Address." *Abergavenny Chronicle and Monmouthshire Advertiser*.

Thomas in Wales, Britain

The family tree of Robert Jermain Thomas

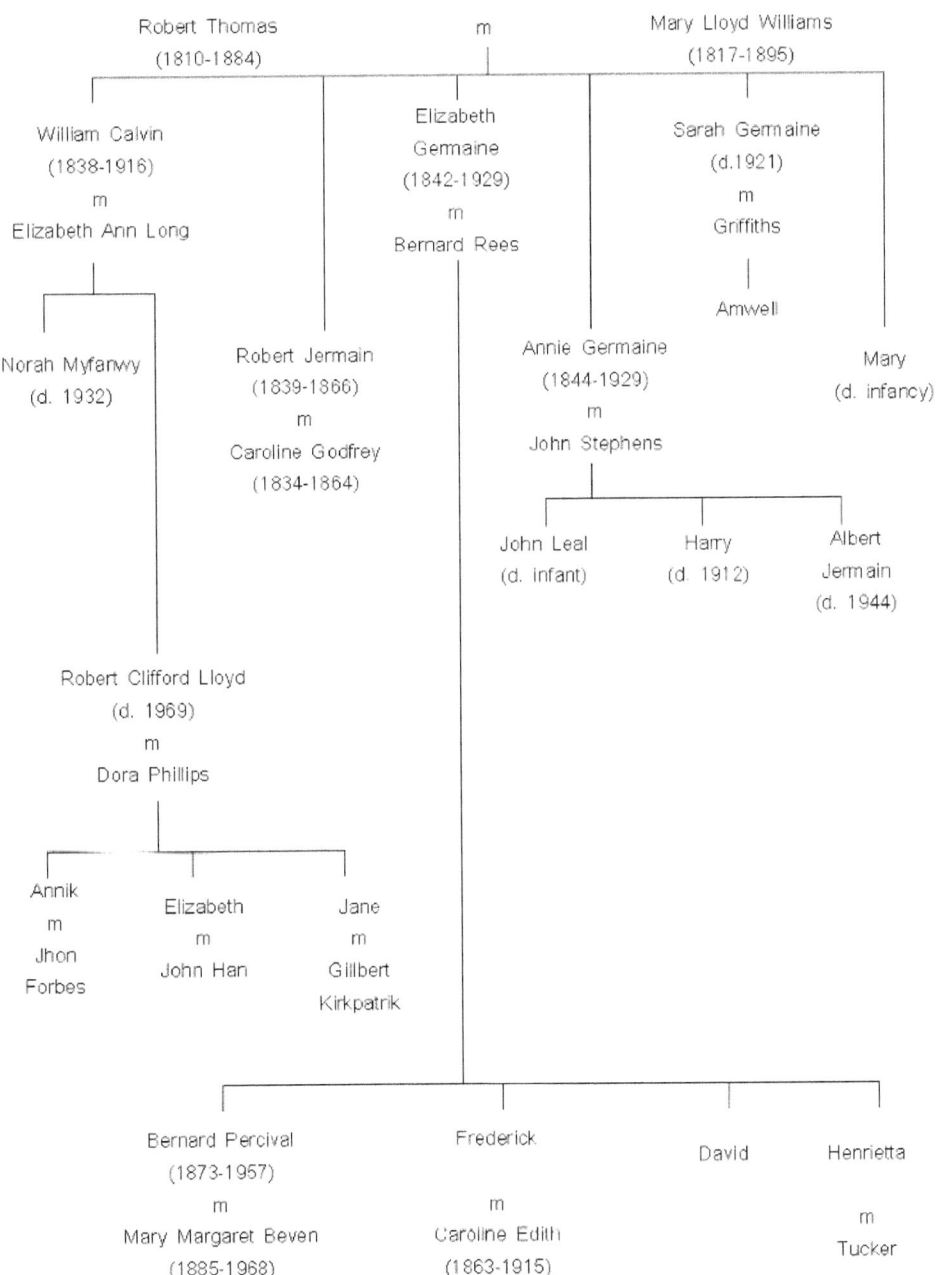

2. BIRTH AND LIFE IN WALES

Robert Jermain Thomas was born the second of Robert Thomas's six children—two sons and four daughters. Thomas's elder brother, William Calvin Thomas, was born in Swansea. Following Robert Jermain Thomas's birth, his sisters Elizabeth Germaine Thomas (1842–1929), Annie Germaine Thomas (1844–1929), and Sarah Germaine Thomas (?–1921) were born. Another sister, Mary Germaine Thomas, died in infancy and was buried in Hanover Cemetery.

There has long been confusion surrounding Thomas's year of birth due to discrepancies in the records. His birth certificate from the General Register Office in London records his date of birth as September 7, 1839,[19] while personal records held by the London Missionary Society (LMS) indicate September 7, 1840.[20] In nineteenth-century Britain, it was not uncommon to register a birthday that differed from the actual one. Such inconsistencies were relatively frequent and not always seen as problematic. In Thomas's case, however, clarifying his birth year carries significance beyond correcting a numerical error:[21] many sources that infer his age at death to be twenty-seven rely on the 1839 datum. Therefore, it is reasonable to consider September 1839—according to the official UK birth certificate—as his correct date of birth.

At the age of nine, Thomas resided with his father in the Hanover Church parsonage. Next to their home was the manor house of Benjamin Hall (1802–1867) and Augusta Waddington (1802–1896). Benjamin Hall was later ennobled as Lord Llanover by the Crown in 1859, and Augusta Waddington served as the financial director on the board of Llandovery College, a prestigious private school in Wales.[22]

Robert Thomas attended a private school founded in 1835 by Benjamin Hall for Nonconformist students. At that time, the school enrolled around sixty pupils. Before Thomas's admission, John Powell had already become headmaster, and Thomas studied at the school from age nine to eleven. At eleven, upon the recommendation of Augusta Hall (née Waddington,

---

19. Certified copy of an entry of birth, no. 153, given June 20, 1985 at the General Register Office, London.

20. Sibree, "LMS Register of Missionaries," 964.

21. Thomas wrote about himself in detail to the LMS on Mar. 8, 1861 and July 12, 1862. His full responses to LMS in Thomas, "Candidate's Answers to the Questions" also extensively explains his life before becoming a missionary.

22. Jones, *Floreat Landubriense*, 334.

Baroness Llanover), he enrolled at Llandovery College—a secondary school (then called a "college") that offered a seven-year curriculum prior to university. His education there was supported by a scholarship established by the school's founder, Thomas Phillips. Thomas and his family were close to the Hall household; their close relationship is also mentioned in a letter Thomas sent from Shanghai to his sister Sarah Germaine Thomas:

> The country around here is as flat as Lord Llanover's pond. Give my kind regards to his Lordship when you go to the next party there.[23]

The church had a parsonage, and in Hanover, there was a mountain visible called Sugar Loaf. In Britain, prior to the eighteenth century, sugar was sold in cone-shaped blocks, which were referred to as sugar loaves. Sugar Loaf Mountain appeared like one of these sugar loaves from a distance. As a child, Missionary Thomas often visited this mountain with his siblings. In a letter he sent to his brother from Shanghai, China, Thomas expressed a desire to run up Sugar Loaf Mountain again.[24]

Thomas studied at Llandovery College under the tutelage of the renowned Archdeacon John Williams (1792–1858) for three years. He graduated early with distinction and, at the age of fourteen, was accepted as a scholar at Jesus College, Oxford.[25] However, at that time, Oxford only admitted members of the Church of England, and as a Nonconformist, Thomas was ineligible to matriculate:

> My education by the late Archdeacon John Williams, carried off amongst other prizes, a scholarship for Jesus College, Oxford. As I was but 14 years old and a dissenter; the scholarship was enjoyed by the second in the list.[26]

After graduating from Llandovery College, Thomas received two years of training under Dr. Waterman, a surgeon. However, his ardent desire to become a minister led him to abandon medical studies.[27] He then accepted a teaching position at a primary school in Oundle, Northamptonshire. This school had been founded by Reverend Alfred Newth of the Congregational

---

23. Robert Jermain Thomas to Sallie, Feb. 4, 1864, Shanghai.
24. Robert Jermain Thomas to Sallie, Feb. 4, 1864, Shanghai.
25. Robert Jermain Thomas to LMS, July 12, 1862, London.
26. Robert Jermain Thomas to LMS, July 12, 1862, London.
27. Rees, *Hanes Eglwysi Annibynnol Cymru*, 35.

denomination.[28] During his tenure in Oundle, Thomas—through his father's assistance—submitted an application in July 1856 to New College, a Congregational institution associated with the University of London.[29] Records from the New College board confirm that his application included the following documents:

> An application for admission on behalf of his son, aged 17 (nearly), was presented from the Revd Robert Thomas, of Hanover, near Abergavenny.
> RESOLVED: that the "Questions" be sent, and the case investigated in the usual way.[30]

However, the university examination board, convened in September, recommended postponing his admission by one year due to Thomas's young age. At the end of 1856, Thomas returned home and began his first sermon at the Hanover Church. The Scripture passage for his sermon was Heb 13:8: "Jesus Christ is the same yesterday, today, and forever."[31] It is recorded that Thomas engaged in street evangelism centered around the Hanover Church until his admission to New College.[32]

In his book *A History of Christianity in Asia*, Samuel Hugh Moffett noted that Thomas was actively involved in his Welsh church community, preaching and dedicated to spreading the faith. Moffett also emphasized that Thomas's experiences in Wales significantly influenced his later missionary work, forming the foundation for his commitment to Reformed theology, which stresses the absolute nature of the gospel.[33]

3. NEW COLLEGE STUDENT

The following year, Thomas took the entrance examination at New College, where each candidate was examined in English grammar, elements of Greek and Latin grammar (with translation), the outlines of Grecian, Roman, and English history, as well as the principles and practice of arithmetic

---

28. Rees, *Hanes Eglwysi Annibynnol Cymru*, 35.

29. Council minutes, no. 133 meeting (July 21, 1856).

30. The father submitted the application on behalf of his son because Thomas was teaching in Oundle at that time; Council minutes, no. 133 meeting (July 21, 1856).

31. Rees, *Hanes Eglwysi Annibynnol Cymru*, 37.

32. Thomas, "Candidate's Answers to the Questions."

33. Moffett, *History of Christianity in Asia*, 45.

and the first book of Euclid's Element.[34] After earning high marks on these exams, he received a conditional scholarship of £40 and matriculated at New College in September 1857. New College, affiliated with the University of London, was founded in 1850 by the Congregational Church. It served as a theological institution connected to the Congregationalist tradition, playing a key role in providing theological education to Congregationalist believers and training pastors.[35]

At New College, Thomas was required to complete the full five-year course while holding his scholarship in preparation for the ministry. After studying for two years, in September 1859, he submitted a leave of absence from the school while residing at King's-Mill House near Wrexham. His decision to take a break was closely tied to the revival movement sweeping through Wales in 1859. Wrexham was near his father's hometown, and the Bethlehem Church his father had attended was still led by Reverend William Williams. It was during that very year that a major revival movement spread across Wales:

> About 110,000 people were converted and added to the churches as a result of the 1859 revival. The Calvinistic Methodist and Congregational churches each received about 36,000 new members; the Baptists about 14,000; the Wesleyans about 5,000 and the Established church about 20,000.[36]

Thomas, having grown up preaching as the son of a minister and aspiring to missionary work, naturally joined the revival movement. The movement was in full swing during his stay near Wrexham. In his March 8, 1861 letter to the LMS, he reported preaching 156 times, specifying venues like Wrexham, Chester, Liverpool, and Chirk, and naming the principal pastors involved:[37]

> The neighbourhood of Wrexham, where I shall reside for some time, furnishes abundant scope for exercising and therefore improving any preaching talent I may possess.[38]
>
> I shall exclusively devote myself to preaching.[39]

---

34. *Congregational Year Book 1859*, 232.
35. Thomas, *Congregationalists and the Church*, 132–35.
36. Evans, *Revival Comes to Wales*, 97.
37. Robert Jermain Thomas to LMS, Mar. 8, 1861, London.
38. Robert Jermain Thomas to New College, Sept. 28, 1859, Wrexham.
39. Robert Jermain Thomas to New College, Sept. 28, 1859, Wrexham.

However, the New College board reacted negatively to Thomas's leave of absence. This was because they had received information suggesting he had taken the leave to work as a private tutor. To ascertain the truth, the board made two decisions: first, to investigate the reasons behind his leave, and second, to inquire about his eligibility to sit for the bachelor's degree examination, enabling him to continue his studies. In the meantime, Thomas passed his bachelor of arts examination and graduated with excellent grades:[40]

> Two sessions at New College have necessarily in some degree matured my views of the Christian ministry and its attendant responsibility. I trust this temporary retirement, which so long as it lasts I shall exclusively devote to preaching, may not render me a workman who is not ashamed of his own deficiencies, but a workman with less [sic] deficiencies of which to be ashamed.[41]

In September 1860, Thomas returned to New College and resumed his studies. Thomas requested early graduation so he could be sent out as a missionary by the LMS.[42] The council reviewed the situation and decided to discuss it with the secretary of the LMS.[43] At this point, Thomas expressed confidence in his ability to acquire languages and was convinced he was ready to become a missionary. Thomas accepted the council's decision that he should complete his studies before departing, and he ultimately finished his coursework. Thomas completed his studies in a total of five and a half years, including his leave of absence. In January 1863, Dean Samuel Newth recommended Thomas for a scholarship, acknowledging his outstanding performance in all subjects:[44]

> The Senate have much pleasure in bearing their testimony to the correct moral and religious character of Thomas, and to his superior talent for preaching the gospel with power, earnestness and effectiveness.[45]

---

40. *Congregational Year Book 1866*, 225.
41. Robert Jermain Thomas to New College, Sept. 28, 1859, Wrexham.
42. Robert Jermain Thomas to New College, Apr. 25, 1861, London.
43. Council minutes, no. 220 meeting, Mar. 3, 1862. Thomas wished to go to China when his friends Mr. J. R. Carmichael and Robert Wilson departed for China as missionaries.
44. Council minutes, no. 264 meeting, June 1, 1863.
45. Council minutes, no. 233 meeting, Jan. 5, 1863.

The council allocated £10 from the Selwyn Fund and £30 from the Mill's Scholarship to support his travel expenses to China.[46] With this funding, Thomas's tumultuous journey through seminary life was finally brought to a close.

A historian, Kenneth Latourette, who called the nineteenth century "the great century of missions," described Thomas, a Calvinist from Wales[47] affiliated with the London Missionary Society, as a missionary who went to Korea—an unknown country at the time—and was martyred.[48] Within the flow of the nineteenth-century Reformed missionary movement, Thomas nurtured his passion for missions with a conviction of the inevitability of mission work and the universal spread of the gospel.

4. MOTIVES FOR MISSIONARY WORK IN CHINA

In his application to the LMS to become a missionary in China, Thomas submitted a letter explaining how long he had desired to be a missionary and the motivations behind that decision:

> I have desired to become a missionary for the past five years. The more settled resolve I date from intercourse with various missionaries who passed some evenings with the students of New College. The first motive that influenced me was this. I thought that men of good education, of strong constitution, with ability to acquire languages were wanted for the work and I wished to offer my services more in the spirit of self-denial than anything else. For the last three years I have deliberately after much earnest prayer, resolved to become a missionary, from an earnest longing for Mission work; the downfall of heathenism, the conversion of the heathen. I do most firmly believe that I am appointed by God to be a missionary, and that He has implanted this preference in my heart.[49]

This statement reveals his unwavering commitment to missionary service. At the young age of twenty-three, Thomas was confident that he possessed both the ability and excellent education—not only in language acquisition but also a spirit of self-sacrifice and a strong desire to spread

---

46. Council minutes, no. 233 meeting, Jan. 5, 1863
47. Latourette, *History of Christianity*, 1189–90.
48. Latourette, *Great Century*, 419–20.
49. Thomas, "Candidate's Answers to the Questions."

the gospel to foreign lands. The motivations that led him to dedicate himself as a missionary to China are as follows: first, Thomas stated that he decided to go as a missionary to China after hearing a sermon by William Lockhart (1811–1896), which was delivered in October 1859 at the New College chapel.

> God implanted in my heart as a result of Dr. Lockhart's speech some eighteen months ago at the college. . . . Over all I have prayed most earnestly for guidance. I am guided to you.[50]

Thomas further explained his motivation to serve as a missionary to China in the questionnaire he submitted in 1862 when applying to the London Missionary Society:

> I must confess, gentlemen, that soon after entering College I did not think much of mission work, was soon however induced to consider the question more fixedly, by a monthly speech of Dr. Lockart. I am earnestly saying of Dr. Legge "that some of the young men kneeling with us may hear and answer the call for help."[51]

William Lockhart was a medical missionary with the LMS who began his ministry in Guangzhou, China, in 1838. Later, in 1844, he established China's first Western-style hospital in Shanghai. He was respected and beloved by both Chinese and foreigners for his outstanding medical skills and character.[52] Lockhart returned to England for the first time on January 29, 1858, after twenty years in China. During his stay in England, he met Thomas at a LMS service held at New College. After about two and a half years in England, he returned to China and opened a hospital in Peking.[53] Thomas continued his fellowship with Lockhart even in China, and when Thomas faced difficulties in Shanghai, Dr. Lockhart advised him to move from Shanghai to Hankow.[54]

The second motivation was the influence of Samuel Martin (1817–1878). While studying at New College, Thomas attended Westminster Chapel in London, a church later known for its pastor, Martyn Lloyd-Jones, who also became well-known in Korea.[55] Thomas was a member of this

50. Robert Jermain Thomas to LMS, Mar. 8, 1861, London.
51. Thomas, "Candidate's Answers to the Questions."
52. Bitton, *Story of Griffith John*, 32.
53. London Missionary Society, "Record of the Reverend R. Jermain Thomas."
54. Robert Jermain Thomas to parents, June 16, 1864, Shanghai.
55. Robert Jermain Thomas to LMS, Mar. 8, 1861, London.

church from 1858 to 1859 and again from 1860 until he departed for China. Samuel Martin provided a letter of recommendation for Thomas to be commissioned by the London Missionary Society. Samuel Martin served as the pastor of Westminster Chapel from 1842 to 1877. In his early twenties, he applied to be a missionary in India but was rejected due to health reasons, subsequently becoming a pastor. In 1862, he was elected president of the Congregational Union of England and Wales.[56] When Thomas left to become a missionary in China, Pastor Samuel Martin personally made him a portable writing desk that could be unfolded and used anywhere. The desk was inscribed with the following message:

> Presented to the Revd Robert Jermain Thomas, B.A., missionary to China, on the occasion of his leaving England, by his Pastor and a few of his fellow members in the church at Westminster, July 20th, 1863—The Lord Bless and Keep Thee.[57]

Third, the LMS had a major impact on Thomas's decision to become a missionary. Founded in 1795 by Congregational churches, the LMS was driven by a strong missionary vision to advance evangelical efforts overseas. In the mid-1800s, as relations with China expanded rapidly after the Opium Wars (1839–1842), the LMS committed wholeheartedly to mission work in China. Its mission extended beyond evangelism: the Society also promoted social transformation through initiatives in education and healthcare.[58] LMS missionaries were primarily based in Shanghai and Peking, where key efforts included Bible translation and the establishment of schools.[59]

Robert Thomas, missionary Robert Jermain Thomas's father, began sending financial support to the LMS in 1842 while serving as pastor in Rhayader. At that time, young Robert Jermain was only three years old. Reverend Thomas was, notably, the sole donor from Radnorshire to the LMS during that period. His contributions continued even after he moved to Hanover Chapel in Llanover. According to the 1868 *Congregational Year Book*, Robert Jermain Thomas had been preparing for missionary work

---

56. *Congregational Year Book 1879*, 331.
57. Oh, "Two Visits," 100.
58. Gill, *Christian Missions to China*, 125–30.
59. Green, *Robert Jermain Thomas*, 50–65.

since his youth, investing all his time and gifts in training to become a missionary of influence and possessing noble virtues suited to his calling.[60]

Thomas grew up in the Congregational Church and attended a seminary founded by that tradition. Lockhart—who also significantly influenced Thomas—was a China missionary affiliated with the LMS. So, it was natural that the LMS would profoundly shape Thomas's trajectory. When he enrolled in New College, London, Thomas explicitly declared his intention to serve as an LMS missionary. He received ongoing mentorship from the LMS throughout his studies.[61] Dr. Robert Halley, who supervised him at the University of London, wrote in a letter to the LMS:

> I can now most cordially recommend him to the patronage of the Society. He (Thomas) has superior abilities and during the last session especially has very diligently and successfully applied to his studies. In his religious character I have full confidence. He seems to have extraordinary facility in the acquisition of languages.[62]

On May 29, 1863, Thomas married Caroline Godfrey (1834–1864), whom he had met in Oundle, at the Kentish Congregational Church in London. The ceremony was officiated by Reverend James Fleming (1816–1879). The following Thursday, June 4, a service for Thomas's ordination and missionary commissioning was held at Hanover Chapel. Reverend H. J. Burn of Abergavenny presided over the service with seven other ministers participating, including Thomas's father, Reverend Robert Thomas. On June 30, the Westminster Chapel, which the couple attended while in London, announced Thomas and Caroline's departure as missionaries to China and held a special time of blessing for them.

On July 21, two months later, Thomas and Caroline departed for Shanghai aboard the *Polmaise* from the port of Gravesend. At that time, there were six missionaries affiliated with the LMS who embarked together.[63] Although not officially LMS members at that time, Alexander Williamson (1829–1890) and his wife, Isabella D. Williamson, also traveled

---

60. *Congregational Year Book 1868*, 298.

61. "Dr. A. Tidman asked—if the council of New College approved, would I go out next July." Robert Jermain Thomas to New College, Apr. 25, 1861, London.

62. Robert Halley to LMS, July 18, 1862, London.

63. London Missionary Society, "Departure of Missionaries for China," Aug. 1, 1863, 250. The content is as follows: "The Rev. R. J. Thomas and Mrs. T., appointed to Shanghae; Rev. J. Williamson and Mrs. W., appointed to Tien-tsin; and Dr. Dudgeon, appointed to superintend the Mission Hospital at Peking, with Mrs. D., embarked at Gravesend, per 'Polmaise,' July 21st."

on the *Polmaise* to Shanghai. Alexander Williamson had previously served as an LMS missionary in Chefoo, China, for six years before returning to Scotland. Subsequently, he was sent back to Chefoo by the National Bible Society of Scotland. In total, eight missionaries set sail on the *Polmaise*, their hearts full of hope for their mission in China.

James Williamson, aged twenty-seven at the time of departure, was Alexander Williamson's younger brother. He had studied theology at the University of Edinburgh and boarded the ship together with his wife Mary, intending to serve in Tientsin. John Dudgeon, a graduate of Edinburgh Medical School, also boarded the ship with his wife Mary Clark to minister in Peking. All of them dedicated their lives to missionary service and were eventually laid to rest in foreign lands.

Alexander Williamson died on August 25, 1869, near Shantung Province en route from Tientsin, after being beaten and drowned by Chinese assailants.[64] His wife, Isabella, had passed away earlier in Tientsin. Alexander Williamson died in Chefoo in 1890, and John Dudgeon passed away in Peking.

Just two months after arriving in Shanghai, China, Thomas sent a letter to his parents:

> London Mission, Shanghai,
> February 4, 1864
>
> My Dear Parents,
>
> You may imagine we were very glad to get your letter, which went unluckily to the French Office here, so that had William not called accidentally, we should not have had it yet. Glad to hear you are all well—hope soon to hear again, longer letters and new.
>
> At Shanghai all is well—to take up the news where my last hurried letter left off. William will tell you all about himself. I am sure you will be delighted to find him so well off. He is quite cheerful, and I hope, in a year or two, that he will be able to send you considerable remittances. Even next year indeed he may send you some, and a trifle of £20 or so thus year. Shanghai is a frightfully expensive place. Everybody says that 1/- in England = a tael 7/4 out here, still, I trust we shall manage alright. If not, we must go to some cheaper spot. William will have to pay us 10 Dollars a week out of his 100 Dollars per month (for the next three months, afterwards more) – a Dollar = from 4/2 – 5/-, subject to state of exchange. William, even then, will only be paying his expenses.

---

64. Hattaway, *China's Book of Martyrs*, 144.

For the last month, Mr. Wyle (of whom I spoke to you as the gentleman who gave me lessons in Chinese in London,) who arrived thro' Russia and Siberia and Mongolia, has been staying with us. He goes away soon to next door (D. Henderson's) as we shall want a spare room. You know he is an Agent of the Bible Society, and will spend most of his time in travelling about up the Tong-tee-Kiang etc. I expected this month to go up to Hankow to see Mr. John, for I have received most kind letters of invitation from him but it is fixed for me to make a trip up later in the Spring. Mrs. John is going to England about April so will stay some time with us here. You must have her at Hanover to give you all the news of Hankow and Shanghai

I think I told you about the rest of our party—Dudgeon, Williamson—off to Tientsin, but ice prevented the Steamer entering Taku, and so put back to Chefoo, and are living in tiny houses—half English-half Chinese—all their luggage in the go down—a most miserable predicament. Alexander Williamson, wife and child, went up to Chefoo some weeks ago, and the Captain of the Steamer made a mistake, ran the vessel ashore in the night—snow two feet on the ground—All the passengers were landed in boats, and had to walk and ride on mules in the night to Chefoo—30 miles off!!! In any case, I am thankful that we haven't to go to Tientsin—Carrie would have been miserable.

We are busy getting our large sitting room in order. Hope to get in it in about a fortnight. My harmonium will be a splendid ornament in it. Carrie is getting on very nicely her servant understands a little English, so as Carrie gets lessons every day from a Chinese lady—they both get on very well. I am very busy all day long. From 7-0 am to half-past—when fine go out for a ride on a little chinese pony—breakfast over a little after eight—Chinese teacher of the Shanghai dialect from 8 1/2 after, walk and talk till then dinner. From 3-5, teacher of the Pekin dialect then a little walk—tea at six from 7-10 twice a week, some meeting takes up an hour and a half, and then read and have a late walk with William. I mix a good deal with the Chinese, and feel myself getting along very comfortably in the language.

Every Thursday evening, there is a sort of address delivered. I have conducted the service once and on Sunday, have preached to excellent congregations three times. Lately a Church (Congregational) has been formed here. For it a new Chapel is being built on our ground. At present, the morning service is held in the Shanghai Library—a fine room, in the evening, in the Church of England. For this year, Mr. Muirhead, in addition to his Missionary duties, takes the pastorate at the salary of at least 1,000 taels about £350. Mr. Muirhead has a wonderful facility in composition, so the sermons, tho' good, don't take up much of his time. The congregation are intelligent and respectable.

We have already some very pleasant acquaintances here. The weather at present is delightful couldn't be better. The small-pox is, however, prevalent, and Miss Gamble the young lady who came out in the "Polmaise" has had a most dangerous attack of it. She is recovering nicely. The Captain and Officers of the "Polmaise" have been up here repeatedly. They are loading cotton, and sail for Liverpool in a month's time.

Carrie can stand the Winter here alright but I fear the Summer for all agree in saying that it is awful most trying, especially to ladies. Fortunately Japan is near at hand in case of sickness.

Best love to Lizzie, Annie and Sallie from dear Carrie and myself. I enclose William's letter.

I am,
Your affectionate son,
R. Jermain Thomas.

Chapter 2

Thomas in Shanghai, China

THOMAS'S LIFELONG PASSION FOR the missionary life led him to China. This vast and unfamiliar country was waiting for the couple, offering a life Thomas could never have imagined. He was to leave China as a missionary, just as he had arrived there as one.

> In addition to what is stated above as to the Missionary's general qualifications I think he should be prudent, self-sacrificing, endowed with indomitable perseverance, that he should avoid the foolish and unlearned questions of the heathen, in chapel and street preaching the simple gospel, that he should watch in all things, endure afflictions and do the work of an evangelist.[1]

1. ARRIVAL IN SHANGHAI

Filled with missionary zeal, Thomas arrived in Shanghai on December 9, 1863,[2] four and a half months after departing from Gravesend. There, he met William Muirhead (1822–1900), the head of the LMS office in Shanghai. Muirhead was delighted by the new addition to the team and quite excited to work with Thomas, who came highly recommended by the LMS. Muirhead promptly sent a letter to the LMS headquarters in London, informing them of Thomas's arrival.

---

1. Thomas, "Candidate's Answers to the Questions."
2. Rhodes, *History of the Korea Mission*, 71.

Mr. and Mrs. Thomas are now with us, and I beg to thank the directors for having sent us such a reinforcement. Your kind expressions in regard to them are amply confirmed in our view; and it will give me the utmost pleasure to labour with our dear Brother in the service of our blessed Lord and Master.[3]

Muirhead, a Scot, had arrived in Shanghai as a bachelor in 1847. He later married Kezia Mary Evans (1820–1880) in Shanghai. He was a veteran missionary, having undertaken numerous inland journeys for evangelical work, and he served as the head of the LMS's Shanghai branch.[4] After arriving in Shanghai, Thomas sent a letter to his parents, describing his joyful life in China:

> At Shanghai all is well. . . . We are busy getting our large sitting room in order. Hope to get in it in about a fortnight. My harmonium will be a splendid ornament in it. Carrie is getting on very nicely—her servant understands a little English, so as Carrie gets lessons every day from a Chinese lady—they both get on very well.[5]

At the time, Caroline was pregnant. Thomas's letters to his parents contain hints about her pregnancy.

> Alexander Williamson, wife and child, went up to Chefoo some weeks ago, and the Captain of the Steamer made a mistake, ran the vessel ashore in the night—snow two feet on the ground—All the passengers were landed in boats, and had to walk and ride on mules in the night to Chefoo—30 miles off!!! In any case, I am thankful that we haven't to go to Tientsin—Carrie would have been miserable.[6]

2. THE DEATH OF HIS WIFE, CAROLINE

Four months after arriving in Shanghai, Thomas visited Hankow for three weeks, starting on March 11. There were three main reasons for Thomas's trip to Hankow. First, he went to find a house for Caroline to recover after

---

3. William Muirhead to LMS, Dec. 9, 1863, Shanghai; London Missionary Society, "Arrival of Missionaries in China," Mar. 1, 1864, 57.
4. London Missionary Society, "Record of the Reverend R. Jermain Thomas."
5. Robert Jermain Thomas to parents, Feb. 4, 1864, Shanghai.
6. Robert Jermain Thomas to parents, Feb. 4, 1864, Shanghai.

childbirth and to spend the summer months.[7] He had asked Griffith John, who was serving in Hankow, to find a suitable home, and John readily agreed.[8] The second reason was John's invitation. John, a native of Swansea, Wales, was an alumnus of the same theological seminary Thomas's father had attended. He had arrived in Shanghai in 1855, resided there for some time, and then relocated to Hankow in 1861. He started a Chinese church in his own home and completed the construction of a new church on July 19, 1863.[9] Thomas greatly anticipated visiting Hankow at Griffith John's invitation, and this excitement was clearly reflected in the letters he sent to his parents.[10] Thirdly, Thomas harbored a desire to serve in Hankow. He had already expressed his wish to the LMS board to work in Hankow even before receiving his official missionary assignment.[11]

However, just days after Thomas departed for Hankow, an unexpected tragedy occurred: the American missionary's wife, who was very close to Caroline, passed away. Caroline was deeply shaken by this news, took to her bed, and suffered a miscarriage on March 20. After the miscarriage, Caroline left a message to Thomas saying that although she had lost the baby, she was alright and he should not worry.[12] Soon after writing to Thomas, she fell into a coma. Despite examinations by Dr. Henderson and another physician, Caroline ultimately passed away on March 24, 1864. Her last words were, "Jesus is very precious to me."[13] William Muirhead wrote a letter to the LMS, explaining the unexpected and sorrowful news:

> I may state that the immediate cause of Mrs. Thomas death was a miscarriage. The wife of one of our American missionary brethren died about ten days ago, and the news of her death gave a great shock to our dear sister. It did not appear in her outward manner,

---

7. "Carrie can stand the Winter here alright—but I fear the Summer for—all agree in saying that it is awful—most trying, especially to ladies." Robert Jermain Thomas to parents, Feb. 4, 1864, Shanghai.

8. Robert Jermain Thomas to LMS, Apr. 5, 1864, Shanghai.

9. Gibbard, *Griffith John Apostle to China*, 68.

10. "I expected this month to go up to Hankow to see Mr. John, for I have received most kind letters of invitation from him—but it is fixed for me to make a trip up later in the Spring. Mrs. John is going to England about April—so will stay some time with us here. You must have her at Hanover to give you all the news of Hankow and Shanghai." Robert Jermain Thomas to parents, Feb. 4, 1864, Shanghai.

11. Robert Jermain Thomas to LMS, May 15, 1864, Shanghai.

12. Robert Jermain Thomas to LMS, Apr. 5, 1864, Shanghai.

13. Robert Jermain Thomas to LMS, Apr. 5, 1864, Shanghai.

being of a remarkably quiet and pensive disposition, but she told it to a friend that she thought her illness was occasioned by the above event.[14]

On his way back to Shanghai from Hankow, Thomas received the devastating news of his wife's miscarriage from Dr. Gentle in Chinkiang (now Zhenjiang). By the time he finally arrived in Shanghai, Caroline had already passed away.

Until recently, information about Caroline Godfrey in Britain, Wales, or China was extremely limited. The only known facts were her marriage to Robert Jermain Thomas, their journey to China together,[15] and her death in Shanghai.[16] However, additional details about Caroline have emerged from her marriage certificate with Thomas, which is preserved at the London Registry Office. Research into Caroline's life began by tracing this marriage certificate.[17]

Caroline's father, John Godfrey (1780–1861), served as a deacon at the Oundle Congregational Church, where Alfred Newth was the senior pastor. Thomas spent twelve months teaching students at both the church and Oundle Primary School. It's therefore presumed that Thomas and Caroline naturally met through the Godfrey family's involvement in the church. Records indicate that John Godfrey became a deacon at Oundle Congregational Church in 1849, and no other deacons were elected in the following decade. This suggests that John Godfrey played a significant role within the church.

Thomas's wife shared the same name as her mother. John Godfrey was sixteen years older than his wife. Caroline grew up in a large household with several servants, her siblings, and her parents.[18] The fact that her siblings were born in Fotheringhay and Orton Waterville, respectively, indicates that her family resided within the same geographical area during her childhood and early adult years. Caroline Godfrey was baptized on September 13, 1834, at the local church in Fotheringhay.[19]

---

14. William Muirhead to LMS, Mar. 24, 1864, Shanghai.

15. *Congregational Year Book 1868*, 297.

16. London Missionary Society, "Death of Mrs. Thomas," July 1, 1864, 220.

17. Certified copy of an entry of marriage given Sept. 2010 at the General Register Office, London. Application number 2566335/1.

18. Tansor Census 1861, the document searched has the reference: M372.

19. Baptisms solemnized in the Parish of Fotheringhay in the County of Northamptonshire in the 1834, Northamptonshire Record Office, M629, Fotheringhay Bishop's

While systematic birth date records were not common during this period, baptisms typically occurred within a few weeks of birth. This suggests that Caroline Godfrey was born in late August or early September of 1834. This date aligns with census records, which surveyed her age in March and April, respectively. Caroline would have been twenty-eight years old when she married Thomas. John Godfrey passed away at the age of eighty-one, eight months after his daughter Caroline's death, and was buried in the Oundle Church cemetery.[20]

Thomas sent a letter to his parents requesting that a worthy tombstone for his wife be sent to Shanghai. He requested that the epitaph should not be altered or augmented, and that her tombstone be plain but elegant, with the letters and shape in the Gothic style. Additionally, an ecclesiastical cross should be added to it.[21]

In his first official letter to the LMS, he reported his wife's death and openly expressed his profound distress.[22] Despite this painful situation, Thomas remained keenly aware of his responsibilities as a missionary. He understood that a missionary needed strong physical stamina and a spirit of self-denial.[23]

That July, an article concerning Caroline's death was also published in the LMS's magazine in England:

> Mrs. Thomas, with her husband the Revd Thomas, had only very recently arrived in Shanghai, their appointed sphere of labour in China, when, after a brief illness, she entered upon her rest and reward on the 24th March, ult. Our departed friend left England with a heart full of love and compassion for the heathen, and though denied the privilege of carrying out her benevolent object, it will console her bereaved husband to reflect that she now serves God in His temple above, without alloy, and without end.[24]

In a letter from Thomas to the LMS, he details how he is doing in the wake of his wife's death:

Transcripts.

20. The text of the tombstone: "In Affectionate Remembrance of John Godfrey whose Remains here lie in peaceful hope of a Resurrection to Eternal Life. He died Nov 8 1861 Aged 81 Years."
21. Robert Jermain Thomas to parents, Jan. 27, 1866, Peking.
22. Robert Jermain Thomas to LMS, Apr. 5, 1864, Shanghai.
23. Thomas, "Candidate's Answers to the Questions."
24. LMS, *Evangelical Magazine and Missionary Chronicle*, July 1, 1864, 500.

Thomas in Shanghai, China

London Mission, Shanghai
April 5, 1864

My dear Dr. Tidman,

I little thought when we left England that the first letter from myself to you, would contain the mournful tidings it now falls to my lot to communicate. My dear wife died on the 24th of last month. The event has quite prostrated me. It was so utterly unexpected.

The voyage agreed uncommonly well with her; hitherto the climate of Shanghai has been temperate and pleasant. Yet immediately after landing the place did not seem to agree with my dear wife. I had no fears, for on the whole she was happy and comforting. True I had fears about the hot weather and the 24th of last month I had taken a free passage to Hankow to arrange if possible that my wife might spend the summer there. Mr. John was exceedingly kind, assured me (as did others) that Hankow was far healthier than Shanghai.

I returned as speedily as possible without the slightest inkling of the sad event that had taken place in my absence. The sad news met me at Chinkiang, communicated most kindly and feelingly by Dr. Gamble. While in Hankow I had a letter from my wife, quite quiet and happy as usual, no one to reckon by, no presentiment. A few days before her death, she, it appears, was shocked by the news of the death of the beloved wife of an American Missionary residing here. That shock brought on a miscarriage which took place on the 20th inst. Afterwards she got on so well that a note was sent to me by a friend telling me not to be alarmed at all. However I had started from Hankow before getting the note.

Monday morning she began to sink; Tuesday nearly all day was unconscious; towards morning Dr. Henderson in company with Dr. Gibbold told me, and now she was awakening, her last moments had been spent in Jesus about 1 o'clock a.m. 24th inst. She was quite conscious at last and her last words were "Jesus is very precious to me."

My heart is well nigh broken. I must seek somewhere a complete change. All that could be done was, I believe was done for my dear wife. Dr. and Mrs. Muirhead and Miss Gamble have earned my deepest gratitude. I cannot write any more; my sorrow bursts forth afresh as I go over the details. I must, to save myself, more completely than ever in the noble work on which I have just entered, but at present I feel weighed down by deep grief.

I am sure I have your sympathy and prayers, that no trial however grievous should separate me from the glorious cause, but rather thank God for the peaceful calmness, and say, The Lord have, the Lord hath taken away, blessed be the name of the Lord.

With kindest regards to yourself and Mr. Prout,
I am, my dear Dr. Tidman,
Very sincerely Yours,
R. Jermain Thomas

3. RESIGNATION FROM THE LMS

For eight months after Caroline's death, Thomas remained based in Shanghai, working as a colporteur. He distributed Bibles to the Chinese people, receiving Scriptures from the National Bible Society of Scotland (hereafter NBSS), where Alexander Williamson served as the China director. However, on December 8, 1864, Thomas submitted his resignation to the LMS. His resignation stemmed from three main factors:

1) Issue of Mission Field Transfer

Thomas wanted to leave Shanghai and serve in Hankow. This wasn't a decision he made upon arriving in Shanghai; he had already requested this from the LMS even before departing London. Later, Thomas sent a direct letter from Shanghai, reiterating his request to be assigned to Hankow:

> You will remember that in my interviews with you in London when for a time my destination was uncertain, I begged, if it were judged fitting, that my destination should be Hankow. This is the petition of this letter. . . . I do not like Shanghai for mission work. It is the opinion of Mr. John (naturally) Mr. Lockhart and even of Mr. Muirhead that a station should be opened at Wuchang and that an application to you be made to appoint a resident *single* missionary there. I earnestly entreat that your choice may fall upon me.[25]

Griffith John was aware of Thomas's eagerness to serve in Hankow, but he couldn't accept him without authorization from the LMS Board.[26]

---

25. Robert Jermain Thomas to LMS, May 15, 1864, Shanghai. Thomas's italics.

26. In his letter to the LMS, William Muirhead explained why Thomas could not go to Hankow: "Mr. Griffith John urged him to abide by that request, and refused to sanction his (Thomas) going to Hankow without the authority of the directors, and in the event of Dr. Wells proving to be an efficient, useful missionary he did not see it at all

Given the circumstances at the time, Thomas's request was reasonable.[27] Griffith John, based in Hankow, had sent his assistant, Lee, to Wuchang,[28] near Hankow, to preach the gospel in 1862, and by 1864, he had purchased land to construct a building there:

> I have bought a piece of ground in the city of Wuchang for the Society. The ground is on one of the principal streets and is about 60 feet wide and 160 feet deep. On this I hope to be able to put up suitable buildings after the festivities of the New Year are over.[29]

A missionary was needed to serve in Wuchang. Furthermore, Wuchang's proximity to Hankow meant Thomas could lead the ministry there under Griffith John's supervision.[30] However, Thomas's request was denied because the LMS considered Shanghai to be the central hub for their work in China.[31]

2) Conflict with Muirhead

The conflict between Thomas and Muirhead is clearly detailed in letters Muirhead sent to the LMS. Thomas also meticulously documented and sent his account of the situation. Analyzing their correspondence reveals that first, the core of their dispute revolved around Thomas's salary. Thomas had an agreement with the LMS to receive £600 quarterly (a minimum of £1,500 annually).[32] However, Muirhead pressured him, threatening to withhold his salary if Thomas refused to preach at Union Chapel, a church Muirhead pastored.

---

necessary for Mr. Thomas to be associated with him" (William Muirhead to LMS, Dec. 8, 1864, Shanghai).

27. Hankow and Wuchang belonged to the mission territory of the same mission society. Kenneth S. Latourette wrote that "the LMS reached out into both Central and North China. In 1861 Griffith John and a colleague inaugurated the first continuing mission in Hankow. Under John's vision and energetic initiative his society reached into the neighbouring Wuchang and Hanyang" (Latourette, *History of the Expansion of Christianity*, 315).

28. Wuchang, along with Hankow and Hanyang, made up the city of Wuhan, which is currently the capital of Hubei Province.

29. Gibbard, *Griffith John Apostle to China*, 77.

30. Robert Jermain Thomas to LMS, May 15, 1864, Shanghai.

31. Latourette, *History of the Expansion of Christianity*, 303–4.

32. Robert Jermain Thomas to LMS, Jan 31, 1865, Chefoo.

Thomas's position was that he was a missionary sent to evangelize among the Chinese, not an associate pastor at Union Chapel (which primarily served foreigners). He viewed Union Chapel as "Muirhead's personal church," not an "LMS-affiliated" institution, and consequently declined the preaching requests. While he had delivered three English sermons during his first two months in Shanghai,[33] he could no longer comply with continuous requests. Another point of contention arose when Muirhead directed Thomas to work as a teacher at the Anglo-Chinese School, which Muirhead had founded. However, this school did not permit Christian instruction, so Thomas refused the proposal. Thomas stated that he was resigning due to "Muirhead's dictatorial measures."[34] In response to this, Muirhead replied as follows:

> I stated all the Committee could do, was that should a Missionary get to his work or missionary himself, they would "put the supplies, and wait for instructions from home." . . . The difficulty about the money arose from this single incident—the same time I had not the charge of your money. . . . I had no control over it.
> Yet I do most emphatically deny that I threatened to "stop your salary" on that account ought else. Then and there I stated all the Committee could do, was that should a missionary not do his work, or misbehave himself, they could "cut the supplies, and wait for instructions from home."[35]

Second, a significant issue revolved around Thomas's living arrangements. When Thomas arrived in Shanghai, he expected to live in a house built by the MacGowan Company, as he had been led to believe while in London. However, Muirhead was using that house himself and rented only a portion of it to Thomas. The tension escalated as the two families shared the same residence. After Caroline's death, Thomas even gave up more rooms at Muirhead's request. When Thomas's friend, British Officer Wood, visited in his absence, Muirhead treated him hostilely, claiming the house as his own.

Third, Thomas also believed that Muirhead's wife had treated Caroline unkindly during her final illness:

> Muirhead has reproached me with ingratitude on account of their attention to my dear wife when she was dying. I must say that Mrs.

---

33. Robert Jermain Thomas to parents, Feb. 4, 1864, Shanghai.
34. Robert Jermain Thomas to parents, Dec. 8, 1864, Shanghai.
35. William Muirhead to LMS, Apr. 27, 1865, Shanghai.

> Muirhead was guilty of neglect towards my wife when dying and of worrying and harassing her when alive. You can imagine how it tries me to write these things, but I do so deliberately and calmly now.[36]

Anyone settling into a new culture inevitably experiences culture shock. For Thomas, the death of his beloved wife, Caroline, was an especially profound blow. Culture shock refers to the disorientation felt when the familiar cultural frameworks and guidelines one has learned since childhood no longer apply. When all the established benchmarks for navigating life crumble, individuals often experience confusion, fear, and anger.[37] Thomas was a missionary who had received an elite education in England. Even before the shock of his wife's death had fully subsided, he found himself in conflict with Muirhead, who was approximately twenty years his senior and had two decades of experience in Chinese missions, due to Muirhead's dictatorial behavior.

3) Thomas's Missionary Strategy

The primary reason for Thomas's resignation lay in the profound differences in missionary strategy between Muirhead and him:

> I presume you will be aware that my views of mission work differ from those of Mr. Muirhead. . . . The *one great* reason why I have been so desirous of leaving Shanghai is the impossibility of working harmoniously with Mr. Muirhead. . . . I love and respect him but cannot work with him.[38]

What was Thomas's view on missionary work that led to such a severe conflict with Muirhead and, ultimately, to his resignation? Due to his short life of twenty-seven years and the scarcity of records on his missionary activities, there isn't much material summarizing his missionary philosophy. However, we can glean some insight into his views on missionary work through his letters and life.

First, Thomas sought to identify with the Chinese people. While in Shanghai, approximately ten thousand Europeans and Americans resided in the foreign settlement, out of a total population of about three hundred

---

36. Robert Jermain Thomas to LMS, Jan. 31, 1865, Chefoo.
37. Hiebert, *Anthropological Insights for Missionaries*, 92.
38. Robert Jermain Thomas to LMS, Dec. 8, 1864, Shanghai. Thomas's italics.

thousand.[39] Thomas's reluctance to preach in English at Union Chapel and his unwillingness to teach at the Anglo-Chinese School stemmed from his desire to build relationships with the Chinese people and evangelize among them:

> My earnest desire is to live amongst the Chinese.[40]

Living among the Chinese wasn't easy for Europeans, but Thomas showed a strong resolve to do so. Isabella Bird, who traveled through China for fifteen months, offered this description of life in Shanghai:

> Few of the lady residents in the settlement have seen it, and both men and women may live in Shanghai for years and leave it without making the acquaintance of their nearest neighbor. It is supposed that there is a risk of bringing back small-pox and other maladies, that the smells are unbearable, that the foul slush of the narrow alleys is over the boots, that the foreigner is rudely jostled by thousands of dirty coolies, that the explorer may be knocked down or hurt by loaded wheelbarrow going at a run; in short, that it is the one point on which the residents are obdurate and disobliging.[41]

Thirty years prior to the previously mentioned period, in 1864, Western missionaries typically did not immerse themselves directly in Chinese culture. However, Thomas actively sought to live and work among the Chinese people. This unconventional approach is clearly evident in Muirhead's critical letters concerning Thomas:

> He remained apart from the proper work of the Station and satisfied himself with going occasionally to one place where a Mandarin speaking teacher had been appointed to labour.... His love of language and travel has brought him into contact with a number of individuals here and in other places which may subserve his ultimate.[42]

Second, Thomas prioritized acquiring the local language. He believed missionaries needed at least two years living among the local people to truly learn their language and way of thinking.[43] Despite his strong lin-

---

39. Thompson, *Griffith John*, 40–41.
40. Robert Jermain Thomas to LMS, May 15, 1864, Shanghai.
41. Bishop, *Yangtze Valley and Beyond*, 25.
42. William Muirhead to LMS, Dec. 8, 1864, Shanghai.
43. His own idea is that no missionary ought ever to attempt to preach in Chinese before two years (William Muirhead to LMS, Dec. 8, 1864, Shanghai).

guistic abilities, Thomas felt that upon arriving in Shanghai, he wouldn't be able to effectively share the gospel until he had sufficiently mastered the local language and customs. While a missionary could survive in the field without learning the language—for example, by hiring an interpreter or using only the few words they knew—such methods would severely limit their ability to build rapport with locals and effectively spread the gospel. For these reasons, Thomas dedicated himself to learning Chinese.

In his letters to his parents, Thomas laid out his daily routine in Shanghai:

> 07:00–07:30—Go out for a ride on a little Chinese pony
>
> 08:00–12:00—Learn the Chinese language of Shanghai dialect
>
> 12:00–13:30—Walk and Talk
>
> 13:30—Dinner
>
> 15:00–17:00—Learn the Chinese language of Peking (Mandarin) dialect
>
> 18:00—Tea
>
> 19:00–22:00—Twice a week some meetings and have a late walk[44]

This daily routine clearly demonstrated Thomas's dedication to learning Chinese. He studied both Standard Mandarin and the Shanghai dialect. While most Chinese people spoke Mandarin, which was the Peking dialect, those in the Shanghai region used the Shanghai dialect. Muirhead reported the following:

> [Thomas was] in the habit of talking in it freely to Chinamen for hours in his own room.[45]

In his letters to his parents, Thomas explained the purpose of his travels to various parts of China:

> A young missionary travelling about here is considered the best thing possible for he picks up the language much more rapidly and pleasantly.[46]

Consistent with this view of missionary work, Thomas dedicated a significant amount of time to language acquisition. As a result, he became

---

44. Robert Jermain Thomas to parents, Feb. 4, 1864, Shanghai.
45. William Muirhead to LMS, Dec. 8, 1864, Shanghai.
46. Robert Jermain Thomas to LMS, June 16, 1864, Shanghai.

highly proficient in Chinese. Pauline Morache, a Frenchwoman who met Thomas in Peking, provides a detailed account of Thomas's perspective on missionary work:

> I met him first in the summer 1864 in Peking at Mr. Edkins where he was on a visit. I was at once much pleased with the earnestness of his principles, the absence of all cant, joined to these frank and gentlemanly ways were his own. At that time already, two or three Chinese told me about his being so affable, so pleasing and how well he spoke their language which is very important thing with them.[47]

This attests to Thomas's unwavering commitment to missionary work, guided by his own principles.

Third, Thomas exhibited a clear focus on inland missions. Church historian Latourette famously called the nineteenth century "the Great Century of Mission" in Christian history. In missiology, the period from 1860 to 1890 is known as the era of inland missions. With the implementation of a more tolerant missionary policy in 1860, missionaries could legally enter the country, leading to a significant increase in missionary activity. Thomas, however, wasn't content with life in Shanghai. He frequently expressed a fervent desire to move inland and preach the gospel directly to the Chinese people:

> The life in Shanghai for a young missionary is not very satisfactory. There are too many interruptions. After spending a few years at Wuchang I should be content to return to Shanghai if necessary. My earnest desire is to live amongst the Chinese.[48]

While he didn't explicitly detail the obstacles in his letters, his concluding remarks suggest there were external circumstances hindering his wish to live among the Chinese. What was the situation like at the time? R. Steer describes Shanghai in his biography of James Hudson Taylor (1832–1905):

---

47. According to her letter to Robert Thomas sent a year after Thomas's death in Korea, she was at Peking when Thomas carried out his mission work. Pauline Morache's letter says that Thomas kept close acquaintance with her son, the doctor at the French Embassy, and that Thomas was diligent with a likable personality. She recalled her time with Thomas in Chefoo before his departure to Korea and wrote a long letter to comfort Robert Thomas on the death of his son. Letters from Pauline Morache to Robert Thomas, 1867.

48. Robert Jermain Thomas to LMS, May 15, 1864, Shanghai.

Many Europeans lived in luxury in Shanghai at this time; it was a new world to western enterprise. Even some of the missionaries were, in Taylor's eyes, "worldly"; they were in great demand with government officials as interpreters and came into frequent contact with officers from gunboats stationed at Shanghai to protect the international settlement. The general atmosphere of hearty sociability came as something of a surprise to the child of a strict Methodist upbringing.[49]

Hudson Taylor personally experienced this atmosphere in Shanghai in 1857. When Thomas arrived in Shanghai six years later, in 1863, the situation hadn't significantly changed. Taylor felt limited in his ability to spread the gospel inland from Shanghai, eventually leading him to establish the China Inland Mission (CIM) in 1865 to evangelize in China's interior. The first principle of the China Inland Mission's manifesto was to prioritize evangelizing in interior provinces that had not yet been reached by Christianity.[50] Younger missionaries, like Hudson Taylor and Thomas, shared this desire to go into China's interior and preach the gospel.

As mentioned earlier, after visiting Hankow, Thomas stayed in Wuchang for two to three weeks in May. In July, he traveled to Peking, then passed through Chefoo before returning to Shanghai. In November, he visited Soochow (now Suzhou), located about 128 kilometers from Shanghai.[51] He constantly ventured inland, serving as a colporteur and distributing Bibles.

Missionaries living in foreign settlements could easily fall prey to ethnocentrism. Western missionary organizations conducted their activities based on common faith confessions, fundamental doctrines, and missionary philosophies, regardless of race, culture, or denomination. However, these Western ways of thinking, despite their intentions, sometimes tended to prioritize Western ethics.[52] When ethnocentrism shifts into cultural relativism, it can create an artificial value system within newly formed Christian communities. In other words, missionaries serving in different cultures need to make an effort to understand indigenous characteristics. In this sense, Thomas's efforts to move beyond the foreign community and live among the Chinese were a pioneering strategy within his historical context.

49. Steer, *J. Hudson Taylor*, 62.
50. Kim, *Jungguk Gaesingyosa*, 30.
51. William Muirhead to LMS, Oct. 25, 1864, Shanghai.
52. Kim, *Seongyo wa Munhwa*, 141.

At that time, China's situation had shifted significantly after the signing of treaties, like the Treaty of Tientsin and the Convention of Peking, with Western powers. Foreigners were granted the freedom to travel inland beyond the treaty ports. In essence, conditions were now ripe for missionaries to freely spread the gospel in the provinces. Thomas had become a missionary specifically to evangelize among the Chinese, so his approach of seeking to live among them was a very wise and thoughtful missionary strategy. However, Muirhead disagreed with Thomas's approach to missionary work. Consequently, Thomas decided to leave Shanghai, unsure of where he would go next. During this difficult period, the LMS remained silent, offering no alternative mission fields. As a result, Thomas submitted his resignation as a last resort.

Thomas's resignation from the LMS was not due to any personal failing on his part. Some of history's greatest missionaries also resigned from their respective mission organizations. For instance, Karl F. A. Gutzlaff (1803–1851) and David Livingstone (1813–1873) resigned from the LMS, and Hudson Taylor resigned from the Chinese Evangelization Society. These missionaries subsequently pursued their work independently.

Such missionaries are not criticized for rashness; instead, it's more crucial to understand *why* they resigned. In Thomas's case, he resigned to draw closer to the Chinese people and to evangelize in the interior. While many considered Thomas's resignation from the LMS to be hasty, few criticized the resignation itself, apart from those close to Muirhead. Later, an investigation by the LMS led Dr. Joseph Mullens to send a report concluding the following:

> His comment on the difficulties at Shanghai—referring to Muirhead—
> That dictatorial spirit is responsible for at least half of Mr. Thomas' vagaries; and many others before him have complained of the same.[53]

Mullens's evaluation of Muirhead, who began his missionary work in Shanghai in 1847 and became the head of the LMS mission there, justifies Thomas's decision to resign from the LMS.

---

53. Joseph Mullens to LMS, Nov. 17, 1865. See also Joseph Mullens's Deputation to India and China-letters, Home Odds-letter no. 11, Shanghai, in London Missionary Society, "Record of the Reverend R. Jermain Thomas."

Thomas in Shanghai, China

London Mission, Shanghai
December 8, 1864

My dear Dr. Tidman,

It is with the greatest sorrow that I pen the following lines. They shall be brief, for I have an unconquerable aversion to publishing any private quarrels or unseemly disagreements of a Mission.

I presume you will be aware that my views of Mission work differ from those of Mr. Muirhead. Whilst all along there has been forbearance on his part and respect for his personal character, on mine still occasionally outbursts of feeling have taken place which have necessarily interfered with that harmony which should prevail between missionaries living under the same roof.

Owing however to recent uncalled for, unauthorised dictatorial measures adopted by Mr. Muirhead and the vain hope of being removed to a more congenial station I must beg to tender my resignation. It has been already tendered and accepted by your Local Committee.

I am bitterly sorry to feel compelled to take this step. I have been treated so kindly and honourably by the Directors and Secretaries of the L.M.S. that now to desert the Society is to me, God knows, a source of deep grief.

From my heart I can say that I came out to China with the purest and most earnest determination to spend my life in the glorious cause. The year I have passed through has been of course one of inactivity in direct mission work owing to my ignorance of the language.

With all modesty I may state that competent judges have told me, that no missionary who has come to China, has, in the same space of time made better progress than I have done. Mr. Muirhead will accuse me before you of all the time hanging about other apparently more attractive visits of labour, and persistently neglecting that where under Providence I have been stationed by the Directors. To this I reply, that I have not for a long time curiously to be removed from this sphere, and when Mr. Muirhead says himself that there are many other fields more attractive on account of dialect or salubrity or peculiar constitution of inhabitants.

The one great reason why I have been so desirous of leaving Shanghai is the impossibility of working harmoniously with Mr. Muirhead. Every missionary of your Society (and many others) not excluding John (tho this last week he seems to have allowed disgust at our disagreements to change his views somewhat suddenly) have approved of my cautious neutrality in reference to Mr.

Muirhead. It cuts me to the heart to be writing anything against him. I love and respect him but cannot work with him. I am sure you have wished to do so, but after a twelvemonth's irregular trial I feel that I cannot brook the treatment that always has been and always, I fear, will be in store for his colleague.

I will say no more. If it is your wish that I should enter into more details in this unhappy affair I am quite willing to do so at once. I shall enter no other Society. I pledge myself as a gentleman to reimburse all expenses incurred by your Society in sending me out and keeping me here.

I take no salary from henceforth.

I beg to apologize for the unconnectedness or rather incoherence of this letter. I have been suffering for the last month from ill health.

Believe me, dear Dr. Tidman,
Very sincerely yours,
R. Jermain Thomas

Chapter 3

Settling and New Opportunities in Chefoo

THOMAS'S MINISTRY IN SHANGHAI was nothing like he had expected. He had never imagined the reasons and process that would lead him to relocate, nor that Chefoo would become a land opening the way for him as a missionary to Korea.

1. INTRODUCTION TO CHEFOO

Chefoo served as the closest port to Korea and played a crucial role in Thomas's journey to Korea. Located approximately 150 miles from Korea's west coast,[1] it was from Chefoo that Thomas first became aware of Korea, met Koreans, and began learning their language. These early experiences shaped his vision of what he called "a country utterly unknown to any"[2]—Korea. According to Min Kyung-bae's hypothesis, Thomas likely first learned about Korea while studying at New College in London.

> It is also possible that Thomas' desire for China mission was influenced by Karl Gützlaff's book that he read in the library of New College. Karl Gützlaff's book, Journey of three Voyages along the Coast of China in 1831, 1832 and 1833 with the Notices of Siam, Corea and the Loo-choo Island was stocked in Homerton College, the branch of New College, in 1836. The book has numerous

---

1. Griffis, *Corea, the Hermit Nation*, 393, in the map.
2. Robert Jermain Thomas to LMS, Jan 12, 1866, Peking.

underlines[3] on Shenzen and Korea. I presume that Thomas was one of the students who took the book seriously. In the preface of the book, Karl Gützlaff touches hearts of seminary students profoundly.[4]

This approach remains conjectural, as it has not been substantiated. Had it been true, Thomas would likely have mentioned Korea at least once in his early letters—but while he does refer to Japan, there's not a single mention of Korea. It's possible that Thomas was entirely unaware of Korea's existence. Yet it's clear that he learned about Korea in Chefoo. After his first mission trip to Korea, all three letters he sent to the LMS include references to Korea.

The name "Chefoo" (literally "signal tower") derives from coastal watchtowers built in the fifteenth century to guard against Japanese pirates. The port was occupied by Anglo-French forces in 1860 and later opened as a treaty port for international trade in 1863.

> The response of Europe and America to the new opportunities was immediate. Almost every missionary society seemed ready to send workers to China, and almost all of them wished to be represented in each of the six locations, which were open to residence. The London Missionary Society and the Chinese Missionary Society both came in force, to be followed by the Methodists and the Presbyterians; of the Americans, the Board of Commissioners (Congregationalist), the Presbyterians, the Baptists, the Methodists, and Episcopalians were established within a few years of the signing of the treaty.[5]

The National Bible Society of Scotland was established in Chefoo in 1863.

---

3. Homerton was one of the precursors of New College. See Nuttall, *New College, London*.

4. Min Gyeong-bae, *Kyohoe-wa Minjok*, 50.

5. Neill, *History of Christian Missions*, 240.

Settling and New Opportunities in Chefoo

2. REASONS FOR RELOCATING TO CHEFOO

1) Alternative Financial Support

Thomas set sail on the *Valetta* on December 17, 1864, arriving in Chefoo on January 15, 1865, to work as an assistant interpreter for Chinese customs. The primary reason for this trip was financial; having resigned from the LMS, he needed to replace the financial support he had been receiving from them:[6]

> We parted in a most friendly way. He has promised to refund the Society all the expenses he has incurred and hopes to identify himself as much as possible with missionary operations in his future course.[7]

Essentially, Thomas had to repay the annual sum he'd received from the LMS in Shanghai. He sent the money he earned from Chinese customs to his parents in Wales,[8] with the specific purpose of reimbursing the LMS:

> I fear the cheque for T. 100 = £33 etc. will not reach you till you get this letter. It's very difficult to send money from here. I tried to send it nearly two months ago. I hope you will receive it alright.[9]

Thomas was always transparent about his financial matters. When he first visited Korea, he declined the commission offered as an agent for the NBSS, accepting only a small sum for travel expenses.[10] On his second visit, although he was supposed to travel as an interpreter for the French fleet, he refused any advance payment for travel costs.[11] Thomas didn't receive any financial assistance for his second visit to Korea, covering all expenses himself. A comprehensive evaluation of his letters and accounts

---

6. The fact that Thomas reimbursed his compensation during his stay is recorded in "Minutes of the Eastern Committee of LMS." "Foreign secretary reported that the Revd Thomas had resigned his connection with the Society, but that he had engaged to repay the total amount of expenses incurred by the Society in his account" (London Missionary Society, "Minutes of Eastern Committee, China," Mar. 14, 1865, 95).
7. William Muirhead to LMS, Dec. 20, 1864, Shanghai.
8. Robert Jermain Thomas to LMS, Jan. 31, 1865, Chefoo.
9. Robert Jermain Thomas to parents, May 8, 1865, Chefoo.
10. Somerville, *From Iona to Dunblane*, 88.
11. Joseph Edkins to his brother, July 25, 1866, Peking.

from those around him reveals his consistent commitment to financial integrity. Therefore, he took the customs job in Chefoo to secure the funds needed to repay the LMS.

2) Recommendation by Sir Robert Hart

Sir Robert Hart recommended Thomas to work in Chefoo and referred him to the customs in Chefoo for the position of assistant interpreter.[12] Sir Robert Hart began his residence in China at the age of nineteen, arriving in Hong Kong in 1854. He lived in China for fifty-four years, with only brief leaves in 1866 and 1874. As a British diplomat and civil servant for the Chinese government, he served as the inspector general of China's customs service starting in 1863, under the direction of the Chinese Foreign Office. Sir Robert moved to Peking, where he resided until 1908.[13] He met Thomas in Peking in the summer of 1864. He believed Thomas's linguistic abilities would be very useful at the newly established Chefoo customs house. After Thomas resigned from the LMS, Sir Robert sent the following letter to Muirhead:

> I think it due to you as chief of the LMS, in view of my acquaintance with you, to state that I have given an appointment in the customs to Mr. Thomas. . . . I would merely state that while I am not sorry to get so promising a linguist for our service, I likewise think that for a man with any missionary spirit in him, there is an opening in the customs for doing great work in an indirect way, and for influencing a class of mine that is not generally accessible.[14]

A letter from Alexander Williamson to the LMS also indicates that Thomas came to Chefoo due to his connection with Sir Robert Hart:

> Having done so he (Thomas) applied to Mr. Hart, chief of the customs, whom he knew somewhat intimately, and received his present appointment at once. He however assured Mr. Hart that he had not renounced mission work but joined him as a missionary and would hold himself free to leave when his way appeared clear. Mr. Hart cordially assented to this, and in this position Mr. Thomas now stands,—and in these circumstances he awaits your reply.[15]

12. Robert Jermain Thomas to LMS, Jan 31, 1865, Chefoo.
13. *Oxford Dictionary of National Biography*, "Sir Robert Hart," 26:590–93.
14. Sir Robert Hart to William Muirhead, Dec. 8, 1864, Inspector General's Office.
15. Alexander Williamson to LMS, Jan. 25, 1865, Chefoo.

3) Relationship with Alexander Williamson

Thomas and Alexander Williamson became close during their four-and-a-half-month voyage from Gravesend, England, to Shanghai. Later, in the summer of 1864, Thomas traveled to Peking, stopped in Chefoo to meet Williamson, and then continued on to Shanghai. When Thomas encountered difficulties, Williamson was the first to assist him. Having served in Shanghai with Muirhead and Griffith John as a missionary with LMS, Williamson was ideally placed to mediate unofficially between Thomas and LMS:

> I have known him for a long time,—know his views, know his ways, and know his doings. I think he has acted without due consideration in the present case. At the same time I am fully persuaded that he is Christian man, and that he is perfectly sincere in his desire to serve Christ in missionary work. . . . He has very great pecuniary inducements to remain where he is.[16]

He wrote a letter to Muirhead on Thomas's behalf, advocating for him. In a lengthy letter to LMS, Williamson defended Thomas, arguing that if LMS gave him another opportunity, Thomas would be ready to serve faithfully once more—and recommended that LMS consider offering him a second chance:

> Should the Committee leave the way open for him to resume missionary labour and appoint him to any other sphere than Shanghai he will not only joyfully accede to their wishes but will feel thankful to Almighty God for enabling him again to engage in his cherished work under their auspices.[17]

Born in Scotland, Williamson was ordained in Glasgow in April 1855 and dispatched to China as an LMS missionary. He left for Shanghai the following month and served there for two years before returning to England on April 16, 1858, due to declining health. Shortly after arriving in England, his relationship with the LMS ended.[18] Then, with the news of the Chefoo port opening under the 1863 Treaty of Tientsin, Williamson was sent to Chefoo as the China superintendent for the NBSS. Letters Thomas

---

16. Alexander Williamson to LMS, Jan 25, 1865, Chefoo.
17. Alexander Williamson to LMS, Jan 25, 1865, Chefoo.
18. *Oxford Dictionary of National Biography*, "Alexander Williamson," 59:339.

sent to his parents indicate that the NBSS was responsible for funding his Bible distribution work as he traveled through various parts of China:

> As I am always engaged in distributing bills, the expense is, of course, paid by the National Bible Society of Scotland.[19]

It's highly probable that Thomas became a colporteur for the NBSS due to his close friendship with Williamson. When Thomas visited Korea on two occasions, his finances were supported by NBSS. This is why a monument to the NBSS was erected alongside the memorial church in Pyongyang, commemorating Thomas's martyrdom.[20] This support came about because Williamson viewed the mission to Korea as an extension of the China mission, despite Thomas being an LMS missionary.[21]

3. THOMAS IN CHEFOO

1) Interpreter at the Customs Office

After Thomas left Shanghai, the LMS accepted his resignation on March 14, 1865.[22] Though he departed from his position as an LMS missionary, Thomas decided to continue his missionary work in Chefoo and became an important figure, recognized for his efforts. Alexander Williamson, in a letter to the LMS, specifically mentioned Thomas's ministry and significance in this regard:

> At present he was doing work—interpreting despatches—more than equivalent to his salary. . . . The customs greatly need such man, and they are flattering him very much. . . . You know his abilities and temperament. He has made very great progress in the

---

19. Robert Jermain Thomas to parents, June 16, 1864, Shanghai.

20. The memorial tablet church wall read, "To the Glory of God. Giver of Salvation through His Son Jesus Christ. And in grateful memory of Revd Robert Jermain Thomas, B.A., an agent of the NBSS, who while introducing the scriptures in to Korea, gave his life near the spot on which this Church is erected. This stone is placed here by the directors of the NBSS, 1932. 'The blood of the martyrs is the seed of the church'" (Somerville, *From Iona to Dunblane*, 64).

21. Foreign Mission Board, "Meeting Minutes No. 3446."

22. London Missionary Society, "Minutes of Eastern Committee, China," Mar. 14, 1865, 95.

language. And I am fully persuaded that he is a young man capable of doing great service to the cause of truth in this Empire.[23]

While working as an interpreter, Thomas's Chinese language skills greatly improved.[24] He also began leading Bible studies for Chinese people, including one individual named Ch'eng, who wished to be baptized:

> I am grateful to God that at this last monthly meeting of the missionaries of this port, I was able to speak with some confidence of a Chinese in the employ of the commissioner of customs. Ch'eng has attended my daily Bible class for some time. He wishes to be baptized. All his spare moments he delights in reading the New Testament and Mr. Burns' book the "Ch'eng tau ch'i meng" = *Peep of Day*.[25]

The only book mentioned in any of the ten letters Thomas sent to the LMS was *The Peep of Day*. Thomas used this book to educate Ch'eng. This devotional book for pious Christians was written by Favell L. Mortimer (1802–1878) and translated and published in Chinese by William C. Burns (1815–1868).[26]

Furthermore, Thomas regularly attended missionary meetings in Chefoo and remained dedicated to missionary activities:

> The Sabbath Chinese service I take alternately with Mr. Williamson and I, also, have to superintend the English service. So you see my hands are full. I love mission work more and more.[27]

In a letter he sent to his parents from Chefoo, he mentioned preaching in English:

> I had a large attendance in the English church yesterday. I had both to preach and play the harmonium, so rather tired after it all.[28]

Clearly, Thomas was consistently continuing his missionary work, even while serving as a customs interpreter.

---

23. Alexander Williamson to LMS, Jan. 25, 1865, Chefoo.
24. Robert Jermain Thomas to LMS, March 15, 1865, Chefoo.
25. Robert Jermain Thomas to LMS, March 15, 1865, Chefoo.
26. Bae, "Three-Self Principle," 48.
27. Robert Jermain Thomas to LMS, March 15, 1865, Chefoo.
28. Robert Jermain Thomas to parents, May 8, 1865, Chefoo.

2) Reconciliation with William Muirhead

Thomas's departure from Shanghai only deepened the conflict with Muirhead. Initially, the issue remained between the two of them in Shanghai, but over time, it spread among the missionaries—some aligning with Thomas, others with Muirhead—and many letters were exchanged. After arriving in Chefoo, Thomas vividly described this difficult period in letters to the LMS. Upon receiving those letters, Muirhead responded through LMS, defending himself and criticizing Thomas's actions. As time passed, other missionaries in China came to recognize Thomas's passion and faith and sought to help him.

Based on the correspondence between Thomas and LMS—and the letters Muirhead sent directly to Thomas—it's clear they both apologized and reached reconciliation. Over the five months following Thomas's departure from Shanghai, numerous letters were exchanged.[29] Then Thomas sent LMS another letter with the following content:

> Mr. Muirhead writes from his point of view and I write from mine. To his letter enclosed I wrote as kindly an answer and I am glad to say that we are reconciled in word, as we have been long ago in heart. It is needless to repeat to you that I love Mr. Muirhead and esteem him in the highest degree.[30]
>
> Mr. Muirhead and myself have mutually asked each other's forgiveness.[31]

Even Muirhead, who had fiercely criticized Thomas, sent him a letter at the same time, asking for forgiveness.

---

29. The following letters are with LMS containing the two persons' conflict from R. J. Thomas's resignation at Shanghai through May, 1865, when his conflicting relationship with William Muirhead ended: William Muirhead to LMS, Oct. 25, 1864, Shanghai; William Muirhead to LMS, Dec. 8, 1864, Shanghai; Robert Jermain Thomas to LMS, Dec. 8, 1864, Shanghai; Sir Robert Hart to William Muirhead, Dec. 8, 1864, Inspector General's Office; Griffith John to LMS, Dec. 16, 1864, Shanghai; William Muirhead to LMS, Dec. 20, 1864, Shanghai; Alexander Williamson to LMS, Jan. 25, 1865, Chefoo; Robert Jermain Thomas to LMS, Jan. 31, 1865, Chefoo; Jonathan Lees to LMS, Feb. 8, 1865, Tientsin; Robert Jermain Thomas to LMS, Mar. 15, 1865, Chefoo; J. Henderson to Robert Jermain Thomas, Apr. 15, 1865, Shanghai; William Muirhead to Robert Jermain Thomas, Apr. 27, 1865, Shanghai; William Muirhead to Robert Jermain Thomas, Apr. 27, 1865, Shanghai; Griffith John to Robert Jermain Thomas, May 5, 1865; Robert Jermain Thomas to LMS, May 15, 1865, Chefoo.

30. Robert Jermain Thomas to LMS, May 15, 1865, Chefoo.

31. Robert Jermain Thomas to LMS, July 28, 1865, Chefoo.

Settling and New Opportunities in Chefoo

> The only thing I spoke of as lacking in you was a missionary Spirit. I may have formed a wrong estimate of you in this matter, and in that case I ask to be forgiven. I pray that the whole affair may be overruled for good, and may be useful to both of us in after life. God bless you wherever you go and whatever you do. . . . Really on looking at the affair in the light of the past and present I am amazed at its contemptibleness, it is a miserable petty difference between two brethren, who ought to and might have been chief friends in God's cause. May it not be yet.[32]

Through his challenging relationship with Muirhead, we can see Thomas's personal growth.

After his experiences in Shanghai, Thomas's mature approach to ministry became evident in Chefoo and Peking. He took on a leading role, even conducting English services, something he had resisted doing in Shanghai. While in Shanghai, Thomas had clashed with Muirhead over educational matters at the Anglo-Chinese school, but in Peking, he successfully managed the entire operation of an Anglo-Chinese school.

Muirhead also shared the same sentiment about reconciliation:

> All the time there was the most amicable spirit felt and shown between us, and we were living under the same roof in perfect amity and good will. Nothing occurred to disturb our harmony and friendship though there was the painful fact that he remained apart from the proper work of the Station and satisfied himself with going occasionally to one place where a Mandarin speaking teacher had been appointed to labour.[33]

For Thomas, conflict became an opportunity to grow into a more mature ministry. In Chefoo, Thomas worked harmoniously with Alexander Williamson, and in Peking, with Joseph Edkins (1823–1905). The conflict in Thomas and Muirhead's relationship transformed into an opportunity for growth in his ministry.

Thomas's move to Chefoo made his visits to Korea possible. Had he remained in Shanghai with Muirhead, the Korean visits likely wouldn't have happened. Therefore, this difficult relationship can be positively viewed as an opportunity for a new beginning.

---

32. William Muirhead to Robert Jermain Thomas, Apr. 27, 1865, Shanghai.
33. William Muirhead to LMS, Oct. 25, 1864, Shanghai.

3) Rejoining the LMS

After moving from Shanghai to Chefoo, Thomas realized his mistakes and sought forgiveness, while also applying for readmission to the LMS:

> Will the Board forgive the past and receive me back? I confess my hastiness. No low or impure motive led me away. I was rash, too independent and with contrition I say so. . . . These trials and lessons are sent me by Providence and God has given me grace and humility to be sorry for my pride. May he give me strength to be yet his faithful servant. I can join another Society, but I think it an honour and a privilege to be connected with yours.[34]

Ultimately, his heartfelt wish was granted. On August 22, 1865, the board of LMS approved his readmission:

> The Foreign secretary stated that he had received a letter from the Revd Thomas, dated 31 January, regretting his withdrawal from the Society, and the misunderstanding with Mr. Muirhead which led to his resignation. Letters had also been received from Mr. Joseph Edkins, Alexander Williamson, Griffith John, and Jonathan Lees, expressing their regret that Mr. Thomas had withdrawn from the Society, and their strong desire that he should again be received by the directors, in the full assurance that he would prove a valuable labourer in China.
>
> Resolved: to recommend to the Board:—That the resignation of the Revd Thomas be cancelled, and that he again be acknowledged as an Agent of the Society.[35]

Having heard this in advance from Alexander Williamson,[36] Thomas was confident he would be accepted back into LMS. In preparation, he submitted his resignation from the customs house. On July 28, 1865, he sent a letter to LMS along with a copy of his resignation. As per his original agreement when joining the customs service,[37] Thomas provided one month's notice before resigning.

---

34. Robert Jermain Thomas to LMS, Jan. 31, 1865, Chefoo.

35. London Missionary Society, "Minutes of Eastern Committee, China," Aug. 22, 1865, 97.

36. Robert Jermain Thomas to LMS, July 28, 1865, Chefoo.

37. Thomas writes, "I resigned and Mr. Hart gave me the post of *only* interpreter at Chefoo. I can leave this service honorably by giving a month's notice for I am doing full work for my pay" (Robert Jermain Thomas to LMS, Jan. 31, 1865, Chefoo; Thomas's italics).

The enclosed is a copy of my official resignation of my post in the customs.[38] About three weeks ago I wrote a private letter to the Inspector General, Mr. Hart, informing him of my determination to leave the service, whether favourable or unfavourable news should reach me from you. I send in my resignation with the utmost appropriateness now, for there is a gentleman in Peking who will at once take my place.[39]

At the time of quitting the customs, Thomas wrote to the LMS:

I assure you that I unfeignedly regret the false step I took in leaving the Mission service.... If God spares my life I trust that having been chastened by him, I may by His grace, devote myself steadily and lovingly to his service alone.[40]

38. Office of Maritime Customs
  Chefoo, July 27 1865.

  Sir,
  I beg to hand in to you my resignation of the appointment I at present hold in the customs service; taking effect from the 31st. of August next.

  I am, Sir Your obedient Servant
  R Jermain Thomas

  Y L Luson, Esquire
  Commissioner of Customs,
  Chefoo.

39. Robert Jermain Thomas to LMS, July 28, 1865, Chefoo.
40. Robert Jermain Thomas to LMS, July 28, 1865, Chefoo.

Robert Jermain Thomas Trip in China

Chapter 4

The First Visit to Korea

THE EXACT NUMBER OF letters Thomas sent to the LMS from China is unknown, but ten are currently preserved in the LMS archives. Of these, three mention Korea, dated January 12, 1865; April 4, 1866; and August 1, 1866, respectively. Additionally, one of the five letters Thomas sent to his parents, dated January 27, 1866, from Peking, also mentions Korea.

I'll analyze Thomas's first journey to Korea with three main goals in mind. First, I'll examine his motivations for going to Korea and the specific areas he visited, based on his encounters with Koreans in Chefoo as documented in primary and secondary sources. Second, I'll focus on the activities Thomas undertook in Korea. Third, I aim to explore his missionary perspective and strategy concerning Korea.

1. DEPARTURE FOR KOREA

Thomas was waiting in Chefoo to be reinstated by LMS. Although Chefoo was officially designated as a treaty port, it still lacked a formal foreign settlement. Nevertheless, a significant number of foreign merchants lived there. The region exported silk and agricultural products from Shantung province and imported a wide variety of goods via Chinese junks.[1] Korean merchants involved in illicit trade with Korea frequently passed through Chefoo. Records from the NBSS note:

---

1. *New Encyclopaedia Britannica*, 12:837.

> The interest of the Society in Korea dates from 1865, when Mr. Williamson, our agent in China, met two Koreans who had come out of the 'Hermit Kingdom' to Chefoo for purposes of trade. They had to come and go secretly, as contact between Korea and the outer world was forbidden. Williamson found that they were Roman Catholic Christians who, however, were ignorant of any distinction between Protestantism and Romanism, so that when Williamson spoke to them of Jesus, they at once saluted him as of the same faith.[2]

Oh Mun-hwan identified one of the two Koreans as Kim Cha-pyeong, while Kim Yang-sun claimed they were Kim Ja-pyeong and Choi Sun-il.[3] They were Catholic merchants who traveled back and forth to China. It's unclear exactly when Thomas met these Koreans. In a letter to the LMS dated March 15, 1865, he mentioned receiving an invitation from William Swan (1791–1866), a missionary to Mongolia, and stated his willingness to visit Mongolia if the LMS desired.[4] If Thomas had met Koreans earlier, it would logically follow that he would have mentioned Korea, but there was no such mention at all. Conversely, had he met them later, he wouldn't have been able to say "I will go to Korea" before being reinstated by the LMS. Therefore, it's estimated that Thomas met the Koreans sometime between March 15 and September 4, 1865, when he departed for Korea.

> Robert Thomas of the LMS met Williamson at this time and offered to go back to Korea with the two strangers, taking scriptures with him, and acting as NBSS agent in return for his travelling expenses. Williamson agreed enthusiastically, and Thomas went off, carefully disguised. While in Korea he sold many scriptures, and began to learn the language. In time Thomas returned via Manchuria, after an exciting journey.[5]

Transportation for this journey was in a junk operated by Chinese pilot, Yu Wen Tai, who had been engaged in trade for twenty years between Korea and China.[6] Wu Wen Tai was familiar with the geography of Korea. After completing his mission on Korea's west coast, Thomas planned for Wu to take him to the northern part of the country, near Manchuria. On his

---

2. Somerville, *From Iona to Dunblane*, 88.
3. Kim Yang-sun, *Hanguk Gyohisa Yeongu*, 43.
4. Robert Jermain Thomas to LMS, Mar. 15, 1865, Chefoo.
5. Somerville, *From Iona to Dunblane*, 88
6. Robert Jermain Thomas to LMS, Jan. 12, 1866, Peking.

own initiative, Thomas resolved to go to Korea with the two Koreans[7] and propagate the gospel, and do so as an agent for the NBSS after consultation with Williamson.[8] Four days before his departure for Korea on August 31, Thomas wrote a letter to the British consul at Chefoo, requesting a passport.

Since diplomatic relations between Korea and Britain had not yet been established at the time, Thomas could not apply for a passport specifically for Korea. Therefore, Thomas said he planned to arrive in Manchuria first, then travel to Peking via Peichili and Liaotung.

After returning from Korea, Thomas reported the following to the LMS:

> You will doubtless have heard of my mission to Corea. Appreciating fully the difficulties and delays which were to be met before an answer of any kind could arrive from the Society; in conjunction with the Revd A. Williamson of the N.B.S. of Scotland I resolved to proceed to the west coast of Corea, a country utterly unknown to any but Catholic missionaries. I left Chefoo on the fourth of September on board a small Chinese junk and arrived off the mainland of Corea on the thirteenth. We spent two months and a half on the coast.[9]

2. THOMAS'S ITINERARY IN KOREA

1) Baengnyeongdo (White Wing Island)

Thomas recorded that he departed Chefoo on September 4, 1865, and arrived on the Korean mainland on September 13. The direct distance from Chefoo to the western part of Korea is approximately 150 miles.[10] Wu Wen Tai's junk arrived near Jangyeon, Hwanghae Province, about nine days after leaving Chefoo port.[11]

---

7. Latourette, *History of the Expansion of Christianity*, 419–20.

8. Oh Mun-hwan considers that A. Williamson advised Thomas to travel to Korea for mission work. However, A. Williamson had not been adequately aware of Korea until he met the two Koreans with Thomas. So in his case, it is deemed to have been impossible for him to recommend Thomas to go to Korea, a place in danger from persecution. Nonetheless, A. Williamson and Thomas, who had ministered together as a team in absolute mutual trust, must have seen eye to eye with each other about Korea.

9. Robert Jermain Thomas to LMS, Jan. 12, 1866, Peking.

10. Griffis, *Corea, the Hermit Nation*, 393, in the map.

11. Oh, *Thomas Moksa-jeon*, 20.

Records of Thomas's visit to the west coast of Korea are also found in *Gojong Taehwangje Sillok* (The Kings Chronicle of Go-jong). According to a report from naval soldier Yoon Seok-gu on October 9, it stated,

> One Chinese ship came to an inlet nearby Charari with nine Chinese people and one British, who was around 151 centimeters in height with blue eyes and reddish face. He was carrying a pistol on his waist and holding an iron bar in his hand. The British, throwing off a bundle of papers, 16 heretical books and one western calendar on the sands, fled quickly toward the south.[12]

The "British" mentioned above would have been Thomas, and the "heretical books" would have been Bibles. Regarding their stop before reaching the Korean mainland's west coast, Harry A. Rhodes recorded that Thomas's ship first arrived at Baengnyeongdo,[13] a Korean island situated on the sea route between China and Joseon.

Many ships destined for Joseon followed this route. On November 1, 1816, the British naval vessels *Alceste*, under the command of Murray Maxwell (1775–1831), and *Lyra*, commanded by Basil Hall (1788–1844), arrived at Baengnyeongdo.[14] They were under orders to reconnoiter the west coast of Joseon before visiting the southern islands. Later, on July 16, 1832, Karl Gützlaff departed the Shantung Peninsula aboard the British East India Company's warship *Lord Amherst* to visit Joseon. He arrived at Baengnyeongdo on July 18 and then sailed south, reaching the west coast of Joseon on July 23, 1832.[15]

Kim Ja-pyeong was a fisherman from Jangyeon on the west coast. His extensive fishing career involved frequent trips to China, making him knowledgeable about the local geography. Oh Mun-hwan confirmed that Thomas stopped at Dumujin in Baengnyeongdo.[16] At the time, Dumujin Port was relatively secure from the government as it was an isolated area,[17] about nineteen miles from the Baengnyeongdo government office.

On August 10, Thomas journeyed to Pyongyang aboard the *General Sherman*, departing the Shantung and sailing via Baengnyeongdo,

---

12. *Gojong Taehwangje Sillok*, Sept. 28, 1865.
13. Rhodes, *History of the Korea Mission*, 71.
14. Hall, *Voyage to Loo-Choo*, 55.
15. Lee, *Dongyang-ül Sömgin Kwichüllapü*, 56–57.
16. Oh, "Two Visits," 114.
17. Kim, *Seontaekbadeun Seom Baengnyeongdo*, 84.

Chodogot, and Seokdo before changing course and proceeding toward Pyongyang.[18]

Thomas arrived on the west coast of Korea via Baengnyeongdo. In his letter, he mentioned two regions on the west coast and the capital of Korea. These regions are identified as Pyeongan Province and Hwanghae Province.

2) Hanyang, the Capital of Joseon

In a letter to the LMS, Thomas noted that he had intended to visit the capital of Joseon but was unable to due to strong winds:

> The storms that blew along the west coast of Corea this last autumn, according to the testimony of Chinese pilots who have traded with Corea for twenty years, have been unparalleled. I should fatigue, were I to narrate our hairbreadth escapes. A gracious providence preserved us. I had intended visiting the capital, Wang-King, but the Corean junk in which I had taken a passage was dashed to pieces by one of these terrible gales. No life lost.[19]

In his research, Goh Moo-song mistranslated "Wang-King"[20] as "Nang-King," suggesting Thomas might not have known the Korean capital's name well.[21] The pronunciation of this term is "Wangjing," and in Chinese characters, it meant the city where the king resided—that is, the capital. Since Thomas was familiar with Chinese, he used its pronunciation of the characters.

To visit Hanyang, Thomas needed to pass through the Ganghwa Strait and then into the Han River. Consequently, while transferring from Wu Wen Tai's junk to a Korean boat, their boat was shattered by a storm. There's a significant record concerning this incident:

> A boat carrying one westerner and his Korean company was wrecked in the wind wave between Ganghwa Island and Gyodong Island on its way to Capital of Korea. Park Dong-yeb, who met the westerner and Korean people surviving from the boat, saying they

---

18. *Gojong Taehwangje Sillok*, July 15, 1866.
19. Robert Jermain Thomas to LMS, Jan. 12, 1866, Peking.
20. Wang-King is one of several Chinese character terms meaning the capital city where the king resides and governs the nation. In Korean history, Wang-King was primarily used as an alternative name for Seoul (e.g., Hansung, Hanyang, Gyeongseong).
21. Goh, "Western and Asian Portrayals," 22.

would be killed if caught by the government army, led Thomas' company into his home and treated them very cordially. They put off their boots on the terrace stones before conversation with our family members. The westerner spoke some Korean and our family considers him to be missionary Robert Jermain Thomas.[22]

Beyond Ganghwa Island, the distance from Jemulpo, the entrance to the Han River, to the capital was twenty-seven miles by foot.[23] However, the route along the river was much shorter. Thomas, driven by missionary zeal, attempted to visit the capital. Not far from there, he encountered a storm and had to transfer to another ship bound for Manchuria. So, why did Thomas want to visit the capital of Korea?

Thomas had acquired Catholic books on the west coast and wished to visit a printing house in the capital. Catholicism in Joseon saw the beginning of a Korean-French dictionary for future French Catholic missionaries in 1853,[24] and by 1864, two woodblock printing houses were established in Hanyang, enabling mass printing and distribution. These began publishing catechisms and Catholic books in Korean.[25] The printing and distribution of these books were not only tools for spreading the Catholic faith but also had a widespread cultural impact on Joseon society. Having already obtained Catholic books on the west coast, Thomas was aware of this and intended to visit the printing houses in the capital with the future goal of translating the Bible into Korean:

> It is certain the nominal adherents of Catholicism in Corea amount to some thousands. At the capital Wang-Ching, the Bishop had established a college, set up a printing press for native books, and had spent many years in compiling a Chinese-Corean-Latin Dictionary and works bearing on the history, resources and geography of Corea.[26]

---

22. *Kukmin-ilbo* [People's Daily], Nov. 4, 2005. Article of interview with Rev. Park Young-jae, fifth descendant from Park Dong-yeb. The writer met Park Young-jae in Ganghwa Island and verified the story appearing in the newspaper. Park Young-jae himself resigned as a Methodist minister. Park Dong-yeb's offspring still resides in the same house in which he met and entertained Thomas, keeping in store the terrace stone on which Thomas had put off his boots.

23. Cavendish, *Korea*, 36.

24. Dallet, *Histoire de l'Eglise en Coree*, 209.

25. Dallet, *Histoire de l'Eglise en Coree*, 209.

26. Robert Jermain Thomas to LMS, Aug. 1, 1866, Peking.

The First Visit to Korea

Thomas's goal of visiting the capital of Korea was thwarted by the storm. He transferred to another ship near Ganghwa Island and departed for Manchuria in early December 1865.

3) Manchuria

Thomas traveled from Korea to Peking via Manchuria. His original plan upon leaving Chefoo was to work as a colporteur on Korea's west coast, then proceed directly to Peking via Manchuria, for which he had contracted with Wu Wen Tai. However, upon deciding to go to Korea's capital, he transferred from Wu Wen Tai's Chinese junk to a Korean ship. When the Korean ship was destroyed by a storm, he transferred to yet another vessel, continuing to Peking via Manchuria as originally planned.

He left Korea and disembarked at the port of Pitzwo on the east coast of the Liaotung Peninsula, where he spent three days. Afterward, he passed through Gaizhou and arrived in Niuzhuang, receiving a warm welcome from the British consul T. Taylor Meadows. From there, Thomas traveled by horse or cart, passing the northern part of Liaotung Bay and the Great Wall at Shanhaiguan, entering Peichili, and finally arriving in Peking.

Manchuria is as vast as France and Germany combined. By 1860, a total of 214 missionaries were active in Protestant missionary organizations in China,[27] yet not a single missionary was in Manchuria. Thomas recorded his observations about Manchuria in his letters:

> Leaving Corea in the beginning of December I landed on the coast of Manchuria and found that I had only escaped the dangers of the sea to fall perhaps into those on land. You are aware that the entire country of Manchuria is in a state of agitation. Long since small bands of mounted robbers were the terror of the longly highway as of the fareast. Latterly these bands have combined together and assumed such alarming proportions as to characterize the movement a downright rebellion.[28]

The Manchu people residing in Manchuria had coexisted for centuries, conquering and ruling China for 250 years starting in the seventeenth century. The migration of Koreans to Manchuria began in the seventeenth and eighteenth centuries. The Joseon government implemented policies

---

27. Neill, *History of Christian Missions*, 240.
28. Robert Jermain Thomas to LMS, Jan. 12, 1866, Peking.

prohibiting Korean settlement in Manchuria, at times even executing those who violated the regulations. Despite the Joseon government's strict controls, a large number of starving Koreans began migrating to Manchuria in the 1860s.[29] The Chinese government adopted policies actively attracting Koreans for economic gain. When Thomas went to Manchuria in December 1865,[30] he observed Koreans quietly settling there. Thomas was saddened by the fact that there were no missionaries to preach the gospel among the Koreans who had settled in Manchuria:

> The enormous piece of Manchuria ceded to the Czar five years ago by the discomfited Chinese has for its South western boundary the Harbour of Passiet, distant but a score of miles from a Corean town. Already many Corean families passing the Ten-man River have quietly settled down on Russian soil. Alas, the rule of Russia is many soldiers, few merchants, and no missionaries.[31]

For four months, Thomas traveled approximately two thousand miles by sea and land after leaving Chefoo. His journey took him along the coasts of Hwanghae and Pyeongan Provinces in Korea, and after his ship sank near Ganghwa Island while attempting to reach the capital, he continued his travels through Manchuria to Peking.[32]

3. THOMAS'S MINISTRY IN KOREA

Although Thomas's first missionary journey to Korea was not long, he engaged in the following missionary activities:

1) Bible Distribution

As an agent for the NBSS, Thomas distributed Bibles in accordance with its mission.[33]

> They are, as a whole, very hostile to foreigners, but by a little chat in their own language I could persuade them to accept a book or

---

29. Dongbuk-a Yeoksa Jaedan, *Manju Geu Ttang*, 185.
30. Oh, *Kidok Sinbo*, January 15, 1957.
31. Robert Jermain Thomas to LMS, 4 April 1866, Peking.
32. Robert Jermain Thomas to LMS, 12 January 1866, Peking.
33. An extract from the "NBSS Annual Report for 1865," 35–36; "NBSS Annual Report for 1866," 41.

The First Visit to Korea

two. As these books are taken at the risk of decapitation or at the least fines and imprisonment, it is quite fair to conclude that the possessors wish to read them.[34]

It's remarkable that Thomas was able to deliver Bibles to Koreans despite not being fluent in their language. Thomas was also aware that Koreans who received these Bibles could face fines or imprisonment. According to one of his letters, Thomas distributed Bibles to Koreans free of charge. In the same letter, however, he wrote that he sold a Bible to a Muslim named Li Kwo Fa in Manchuria:

> I landed at a port called Pi-tz-Wo, two days after leaving, it was occupied by rebels. I had spent three very pleasant days in distributing the scriptures and preaching the gospel. The people were more than merely civil and attentive. A Mohammedan named Li Kwo Fa bought a copy, of each kind of book I had and insisted on sending me dinner, daily, free of expense!![35]

Did Thomas always distribute Bibles for free, or did he sometimes sell them? Let's look at the history of Bible distribution by the NBSS:

> The NBSS was formed in 1860 by the union of several older bodies, and in 1863 it sent Alexander Williamson as its first representative. Williamson remained with the Society only until 1866, but other agents were employed, the central office was moved from the North to Hankow, and by 1896 nine Europeans were reported on the staff with about one hundred Chinese colporteurs. The original policy of the Bible societies was to distribute the scriptures without cost to the recipients, but in the sixties the conclusion was reached that the Chinese would value the scriptures more highly if they paid for them. Even then the prices were so low that many copies were wasted. The major numbers of the volumes distributed were single books—usually one of the gospels—and not entire Testaments or Bibles.[36]

Thomas distributed Bibles both free of charge and for a fee, depending on the circumstances. In Korea, he gave them away for free. While Thomas was in Peking, the capital of China, he received a note from someone

---

34. Robert Jermain Thomas to LMS, Jan. 12, 1866, Peking.
35. Robert Jermain Thomas to LMS, Jan. 12, 1866, Peking.
36. Latourette, *History of Protestant Missions*, 138–39; *China Mission Handbook*, 2:300.

accompanying the Korean government, requesting a copy of Matthew's Gospel that had been distributed on the west coast the previous year.

> Religious books were distributed by me last year all along the west coast. In January of the year a note in Chinese was put into my hand by a member of the Corean Embassy in Peking begging a copy of Matthew gospel, like that a foreigner had distributed on the coast of Corea. These facts speak for themselves. It does not dissipate our force to extend the influence of the Word of God.[37]

He noted that the Bibles he distributed were widely circulated in Korea and heard that a Korean official even wanted a copy of Matthew's Gospel from him. Thomas was delighted to see the fruits of his labor, having distributed Bibles in a place where there was not a single Protestant believer. The Chinese Bibles Thomas distributed in Korea were New Testaments published by the LMS press in Shanghai, China, in 1858.[38]

2) Acquiring the Korean Language

> We spend two months and a half on the coast. I had acquired thro' the assistance of a Corean Roman Catholic sufficient knowledge of the colloquial to announce to these poor people some of the most precious truths of the gospel.[39]

What motivated Thomas to learn Korean? Firstly, it was to evangelize to the Korean people, and secondly, to translate the Bible. While Hangeul began to be used in all official Korean documents in 1894, Chinese was the common language for the Joseon government and the upper class when Thomas arrived in Korea with Chinese Bibles. For the children of the yangban (upper-class), nearly all scholarly pursuits involved studying Chinese.[40] Moreover, commoners also had a strong desire to learn. Thomas was aware of these facts:

> The Chinese literary style is well understood and exclusively used by the educated classes in Corea.[41]

---

37. Robert Jermain Thomas to LMS, Aug. 1, 1866, Peking.
38. Oh, *Kidokgongbo*, Jan. 15, 1957.
39. Robert Jermain Thomas to LMS, Jan. 12, 1866, Peking.
40. Dallet, *Histoire de l'Eglise en Coree*, 135.
41. Robert Jermain Thomas to LMS, Apr. 4, 1866, Peking.

The First Visit to Korea

However, most lower-class individuals couldn't read Chinese Bibles. As evidenced by his use of the phrase "poor people" in his letters, Thomas collected materials and conducted research to translate the Bible into Hangul so that lower-class people could read it:

> They have however a syllabary for their own colloquial which is universally understood. The Roman Catholics have translated their series of catechism, breviary, etc. into most idiomatic colloquial, using of course the native character. So little difficulty in translating our books into a character and language understood by boys and girls throughout the whole country for the dialectic differences are inconsiderable in the eight provinces.[42]

Thomas kept up his efforts to learn Korean in Peking, aiming to translate the Bible. While there, he heard news of the Catholic persecution in Korea in 1866: all books published by Catholics were burned, and their printing houses and seminaries in the capital were shut down. He reported this to the LMS:

> Last year when in Corea I procured a complete set of these latter works, which will be of great use in the ultimate compiling of purer elementary Christian works.[43]

While on Korea's west coast, Thomas acquired Catholic books published by the printing houses in the Korean capital. His desire to translate the Bible into Korean became evident during his second missionary journey to Korea. Thomas's experiences in Korea were recorded in the 1866 report of the NBSS:

> Sailing along the coast, at considerable risk, he had mixed with Corean traders, and had found some who offered to conduct him to the capital, if he visited them next year; he had procured several books in the native language, and had made a vocabulary of it, till he was able to speak, to some extent, the dialect of the capital.[44]

---

42. Robert Jermain Thomas to LMS, Apr. 4, 1866, Peking.
43. Robert Jermain Thomas to LMS, Aug. 1, 1866, Peking.
44. An extract from the "NBSS Annual Report for 1866," 36.

3) Building Relationships

According to Thomas's letters, he prepared to revisit Korea. In line with his missionary goals, he built relationships with people, anticipating his return to Korea after acquiring language proficiency:

> I am well acquainted with the coast of two Western provinces of Corea and have made numerous vocabularies and dialogues in the colloquial of the capital, which will be useful in any future negotiations with that people.[45]
>
> Whilst in Corea I made the acquaintance of several.[46]
>
> I take a good supply of books with me and am quite sanguine that I shall be welcomed by the *people*.[47]

In his letters to the LMS, Thomas wrote that he would be welcomed by the Korean people. Who exactly did "Korean people" refer to? From Thomas's presumption that he would be welcomed, three conclusions can be drawn.

Firstly, he likely expected to be welcomed by the Koreans he had already befriended. These would have been the individuals he first met in Chefoo, from whom he learned Korean, and who accompanied him to the west coast.

Secondly, it could refer to the people he met while distributing Bibles. Comparing this to his missionary strategy in China, it's highly probable that he formed good relationships with influential people among those he met during his two and a half months there, and if he returned, he would have received a favorable response from them.

Thirdly, it could mean the Koreans he met in Peking, specifically members of the Dongjisa mission who visited Peking and were part of the Joseon government. Thomas had grown close to them, sometimes even promising to meet again if he revisited Korea.

Therefore, it's highly probable that he anticipated a favorable reaction from them upon a future encounter.

---

45. Robert Jermain Thomas to LMS, Jan. 12, 1866, Peking.
46. Robert Jermain Thomas to LMS, Apr. 4, 1866, Peking.
47. Robert Jermain Thomas to LMS, Aug. 1, 1866, Peking. Thomas's italics.

The First Visit to Korea

Wu Wen Tai, the pilot of the Chinese junk Thomas mentioned,[48] also assisted him during his second visit to Korea.[49] Captain R. W. Shufeldt (1822–1895) of the USS *Wachusett*, dispatched by the American government to investigate the *General Sherman* incident, departed Chefoo on January 22, 1867. He took American missionary Hunter Corbett (1835–1920) as his interpreter and Wu Wen Tai as his guide for the route to the west coast.[50] Furthermore, the person Thomas referred to as "the assistance of a Corean Roman Catholic"[51] in his letters was likely Kim Ja-pyeong, who had taught him Korean. Thomas received much assistance from Kim Ja-pyeong, who was from Jangyeon and familiar with the local conditions. Another Korean Thomas met in Chefoo, Choi Sun-il,[52] went to China in 1866 with French priest S. Feron (1827–1903), who had left Korea after the persecution. When investigating the *General Sherman* incident, Shufeldt arranged meetings with French priests F. C. Ridel and Feron and obtained information through an interview with Choi Sun-il.[53] In this way, Thomas built relationships with many people he met, concluding his first missionary journey to Korea by assessing that "the people of Corea, on good testimony, are more accessible to Christian truth than either of the others."[54]

> London Mission, Peking,
> January 12, 1866
>
> My dear Dr. Tidman,
>
> I arrived here a week to-day and only then learned the blessed news that I had been appointed to this most interesting Mission. You will doubtless have heard of my mission to Corea. Appreciating fully the difficulties and delays which were to be met before

---

48. Robert Jermain Thomas to LMS, Jan. 12, 1866, Peking.

49. Pak, *Jang-kea*, Aug. 18, 1866.

50. "Library of Congress, Microfilms, Roll 28299. Abstract Log the USS *Wachusett*. R. W. Shufeldt Esq. 23 January 1865–1868, Jan. 22, 1867," cited in Kim, *Kundae Hanmi Kwangea-sa*, 214.

51. Robert Jermain Thomas to LMS, Jan. 12, 1866, Peking.

52. "Febiger Letters, 'J.' USS *Shenandoah*, Off the mouth of the Ping Yang River, Corea, May 4, 1868. (Febiger Letters, 'I.' Poo Ting Ho District Magistrate of Chung Leen, Corea to Captain Febiger, May 2, 1866," cited in Kim, *Kundae Hanmi Kwangea-sa*, 43.

53. "Shufeldt Letter: USS *Wachusett*, Shanghai, China, Jan. 9, 1867; Shufelt's Interview with Father Ridel and Corean, Shanghai, China, Jan. 9, 1867 (Febiger Letters, 'I.' Poo Ting Ho District Magistrate of Chung Leen, Corea to Captain Febiger, May 2, 1866," cited in Kim, *Kundae Hanmi Kwangea-sa*, 216.

54. Robert Jermain Thomas to LMS, Aug. 1, 1866, Peking.

an answer of any kind could arrive from the Society in conjunction with the Rev. A. Williamson of the N.B.S. of Scotland I resolved to proceed to the West coast of Corea, a country utterly unknown to any but Catholic missionaries. I left Chefoo on the fourth of September on board a small Chinese junk and arrived off the mainland of Corea on the thirteenth. We spent two months and a half on the coast. I had acquired thro the assistance of a Corean Roman Catholic sufficient knowledge of the colloquial to announce to these poor people some of the most precious truths of the Gospel. They are, as a whole, very hostile to foreigners, but by a little chat in their own language I could persuade them to accept a book or two. As these books are taken at the risk of decapitation or at least fines and imprisonment, it is quite fair to conclude that the possessors wish to read them. The storms that blew along the west coast of Corea this last autumn, according to the testimony of Chinese pilots who have traded with Corea for twenty years, have been unparalleled. I should fatigue, were I to narrate our hairbreadth escapes. A gracious Providence preserved us. I had intended visiting the Capital, Wang-King, but the Corean junk in which I had taken a passage was dashed to pieces by one of these terrible gales. No life lost. Leaving Corea in the beginning of December I landed on the coast of Manchuria and found that I had only escaped the dangers of the sea to fall perhaps into those on land. You are aware that the entire country of Manchuria is in a state of agitation. Long since small bands of mounted robbers were the terror of the lonely highways of the far east. Latterly these bands have combined together and assumed such alarming proportions as to characterize the movement a downright rebellion. I landed at a port called Pi-tz-Wo, two days after leaving, it was occupied by rebels. I had spent three very pleasant days in distributing the Scriptures and preaching the Gospel. The people were more than merely civil and attentive. A Mohammedan named Li Kwo Fa bought a copy, of each kind of book I had and insisted on sending me dinner, daily, free of expense!!

Passing through Kaichou I arrived at Yingtsz (Newchwang) where I was very hospitably entertained by H.B.M's Consul, T. Taylor Meadow, Esq. Thence travelling partly on horseback and part of the time in carts, rounding the northern part of the Gulf of Liau Tung and passing the Great Wall at Shan Hai kwan I entered the Province of Chili and breathed freely, for thither the robbers could not follow us. The Chinese Government had despatched some four thousand troops to tranquilize Manchuria.

To sum up I have been four months away from European Society and travelled by sea and land nearly two thousand miles. I am well acquainted with the coast of two Western provinces of Corea and have made numerous vocabularies and dialogues in the colloquial of the Capital which will be useful in any future negotiations with that people.

I can hardly express to you how glad I am to be here. By God's help I will try to bear part of the burden which Mr. Edkins has borne so long and so well. I wish to convey to the Board my grateful thanks for their kindness. Will you too accept my best thanks for the kind, encouraging words you have uttered from time to time pending the ultimate decision of the Board.

Two days ago Dr. Martin an American missionary asked me whether I would consent to take charge of the Anglo-Chinese school attached to the Foreign Office in this city. There are but six pupils who require attendance, of two hours daily and the salary is one thousand taels per annum. I at once declined the offer, but it is my duty to report the circumstance to you. May I ask the opinion of the Board of Directors? Unquestionably it is an admirable school, where a young missionary could not but progress with well in his elementary Chinese studies.

With the approval of Mr. Edkins I offered to assist Dr. Martin, but fearing two opposing systems the Doctor declined. H.E. General Hougoli(?) the Russian Minister urged me to take the school.

The first week of my residence here has necessarily been taken up in making the usual calls on the foreign residents. Our "Week of prayer" meetings hitherto have been well attended.

Next week I purpose commencing in earnest a course of study which will fit me for the Chinese pulpit.

With kind regards to the Directors,
I believe me, dear Dr. Tidman,
Very sincerely yours,
R. Jeremiah Thomas

P.S. May I beg that you will excuse this hurried letter, I do not wish to allow another Russian mail to leave without informing you of my safe arrival. R.J.T.

London Mission, Peking,
January 27, 1866

My dear Parents,

Last week I wrote you by the most convenient mail from here—that is via Russia. It is speedier than the Marseilles mail in the winter time. I wrote also to Mrs. Godfrey. Should any accident or delay happen to the letters, please write & tell Mrs. G. that there is a letter on the way to her. I spoke in my letter of . . . £50 for a tombstone for dear Carry. I think including all expenses that oughtn't to exceed £40 to Shanghai. Should there be £10 spare -after paying the expense of your journey to London etc., to choose the slab, will you kindly buy me four engravings—£1. 1.0 each, with glass & simple but elegant frames and have them carefully packed up and sent to me in a box most carefully packed and addressed to me, care of Commissioners of Customs, Chefoo. I want them addressed to him for Captains of ships are much more willing to oblige Customs Officers than Missionaries, inasmuch as a Commissioner of Customs can oblige them in many ways. And the Commissioner has given me permission to have my things sent to them. Mamma grumbles that I don't write long letters nor acknowledge what you write in yours. I fancy several of my letters must have gone a missing. This last week I received Mamma's likeness. I don't much admire it, but am nevertheless glad to have it. Mamma's suspicions that I am a wandering star are quite without foundation – I travel for my health—it's happily reestablished, now here I intend to remain—the goal of my ambition—you will know that the London Mission here is composed of three—Mr. Edkins, Dr. Dudgeon & myself. I am very busy every day, going on with my Chinese studies, and preparing my rooms. We all live in these large premises. Dr. Dudgeon lives separately. I have four rooms—board with the Edkins. Keep a servant boy (a Chinaman) a groom (a Mongol) and a pony. I am very happy here. But I endured such hardships during my long journey that any place seems comfortable. I have had an audience with all the foreign ambassadors to the Court of Peking respecting my travels. Dined the night before last at the English Legation with the two attaches (Secretaries) of the British Legation.

  I preach my first sermon here next Sunday (in Chinese), on the parable Dives & Lazarus. We have a nice large Chapel in the front of our premises. Last week was a week of prayer. All the missionaries met daily at each other's houses. It is really not an easy task to give details of our daily life here.

We live very well. Dine on venison, hares, pheasants, partridges, beef, mutton, . . . all excellent and very cheap. All frozen so keep well. It was but yesterday that Mr. and Mrs. Edkins bought fifty partridges. We can buy a deer for nine shillings and a sheep for seven shillings.

Then for dessert, apples, pears and grapes every morning at breakfast and evening at dinner. We thus live infinitely better and cheaper than at home in England. Peking is interesting at all times, but particularly now before the Chinese New Year. Mongols, Coreans are pouring in. Mr. Edkins and I have a class of Chinese enquirers every morning. Then after breakfast, there is preaching in the Chapel for three or four hours by the native assistants. Then I go a shopping, or for a ride. The weather is very fine but cold. No snow, but during the high winds, plenty of dust. I hear this post of my luggage left in Chefoo has been stolen, so I have lost about £10 worth of things!!!! But we take these misfortunes very cooly in China. Not long ago at Tientsin in the home of a Methodist missionary named Innocent, the thieves broke in their bedroom whilst they were asleep and stole the time-piece from on the mantlepiece! The fewer things one has the better. I am compelled to spend a good deal just now for furniture & clothes. I get everything made here. I wonder what kind of stuff are made of. John of Hankow is coming up here in the Spring and is going with Edkins to make a tour in Mongolia, The whole superintendence of the preaching and teaching will thus during a month or two fall on my shoulders. I hope William has got safely home again. As I have told you over & over again—if his were the studious & clever persons? . . . owing to the present and for some time past utter stagnation of business, no place could have been got for him. I should tremble at his taking, even if he could get it, a low place. Persons of good education who came to lose situations in China as a rule drink themselves to death. It is a frightful curse drink here. I have seen a whole community of merchants get drunk after dinner, and the next day not feel at all ashamed.

Mamma asks "Where is your" M . . . now". Now I can't read the word tho' I have spent five minutes over it. I only heard by last Sunday's mail that the vessel bringing my books (Spirit of the Days) had safely arrived in Shanghai, but owing to the Tientsin river being frozen, I shall not get the contents till beginning of April.

We are not at all alarmed about the "rebels" here.

I am glad to hear that dear Lallie is better. If a trip would do her good to Torquay or anywhere else, I'll give up my wish for the engravings and let Mamma go with her to Devonshire.

Now don't make any mistake about the taste of tombstone—plain—but elegant—with a cross—an ecclesiastical looking one -. Do not add to or alter my epitaph, and don't say anything about it to Mrs. Godfrey at present. The colours of the letters and shape are to be on what is termed the Gothic style. I expect to send you the money not long after this letter reaches you. Tell dear Annie that before next Autumn she may expect from me as a present a sable muff—of course only the skins made up—she may line it and stuff it as she likes, and Lallie shall have an ermine one. The cap I have on now is made of sable—dear but nice to look at and feel. Now with love again to all, Believe me.

Your affectionate son,
Sgd R. Jermain Thomas.

The Bessie never came nearer than Hongkong. I enclose you William's two letters. Let him know as soon as you can that when his letters arrived at Chefoo, I was in Corea and only received them Jan 5th 1865.

The First Visit to Korea

Robert Jermain Thomas the 1st Trip in Korea

Chapter 5

Peking
A Season of Mission Integration

THE CONFLICTS IN SHANGHAI were resolved as Thomas discovered a new path as a missionary in Chefoo. However, his missionary journey remained unfulfilled. In Beijing, he matured in his calling and prepared for the final chapter of his mission.

1. ARRIVAL IN PEKING

The Convention of Peking, concluded with Great Britain, France, and Russia in 1860, facilitated the establishment of diplomatic legations and the permanent stationing of foreign envoys in Peking. Concurrently, missionary societies commenced new evangelical endeavors within the city.[1] Following a four-month journey from Chefoo, Thomas arrived in Peking on January 5, 1866.[2] Upon his arrival, he was officially informed of his readmission to the LMS on August 22, 1865, and his designation to the Peking mission field.[3] Thomas conveyed his profound joy and gratitude to the LMS in his correspondence.[4]

---

1. *New Encyclopaedia Britannica*, 16:124.
2. Robert Jermain Thomas to LMS, Jan. 12, 1866, Peking.
3. Robert Jermain Thomas to LMS, Jan. 12, 1866, Peking.
4. Robert Jermain Thomas to LMS, Jan. 12, 1866, Peking.

In a letter addressed to his parents, Thomas recounted the arduous four months spent during his visit to Korea, noting his subsequent contentment and intention to reside in Peking.

> Now here (Peking) I intend to remain—the goal of my ambition—you will know that the London Mission here is composed of three—Mr. Edkin, Dr. Dudgeon and myself. I am very busy every day, going on with my Chinese studies, and preparing my rooms. We all live these large premises. Dr. Dudgeon lives separately. I have four rooms—board with the Edkins. Keep a servant boy (a Chinese), a groom (a Mongol) and a pony. I am very happy here. I have had an audience with all the foreign ambassadors to the Court of Peking respecting my travels. Dined the night before last at the English Legation with the two attaches (Secretaries) of the British Legation.[5]

Thomas studied Chinese using a book authored by Joseph Edkins (1823–1905) in England. In a letter to the LMS dated December 23, 1862, he reported purchasing Edkins's *Grammar of the Mandarin Dialect*.[6] Joseph Edkins, regretting Thomas's departure from the LMS, had sent him a letter stating he would be welcomed back if readmitted and assigned to Peking.[7] Now, having arrived in Peking and looking forward to ministering alongside Edkins, Thomas expressed his gratitude and greetings, revealing his determination to share the burdens of missionary work:

> I can hardly express to you how glad I am to be here. By God's help I will try to bear part of the burden which Mr. Edkins has borne so long and so well.[8]

2. MINISTRY IN PEKING

Upon his arrival in Peking, Thomas began preaching in Chinese on the parable of the rich man and Lazarus during his first Sunday at the LMS chapel in Peking.[9] One of Thomas's most important daily routines was attending

---

5. Robert Jermain Thomas to parents, Jan. 27, 1866, Peking.
6. Robert Jermain Thomas to LMS, Dec. 23, 1862, London.
7. Robert Jermain Thomas to LMS, Mar. 15, 1865, Chefoo.
8. Robert Jermain Thomas to LMS, Jan. 12, 1866, Peking.
9. Robert Jermain Thomas to parents, Jan. 27, 1866, Peking.

the LMS worship service every morning and preaching for three to four hours to the Chinese visitors there:

> Mr. Edkins and I have a class of Chinese enquirers every morning. Then after breakfast, there is preaching in the chapel for three or four hours by the native assistants.... We have a nice large chapel in the front of our premises.[10]

His experience in Shanghai became a driving force for Thomas to continue a mature missionary ministry. His collaboration with Edkins and Chinese workers was yielding tangible results. Thomas's ministry is detailed in a letter from Pauline Morache, a French national who accompanied him on his journey from Peking to Chefoo:

> A daily and regular preaching from 10 in the morning till 4 in the afternoon. Between 50–100 Chinese, changing now and then, sat listening the gospel, some patiently, some earnestly, everyone decent while coming sitting or going. Besides these daily evangelical exercises, there was Divine Service in three different chapels on Sabbath. At these preachings were afforded only Mr. Edkins, your son and several Chinese catechists. It is a fact that they had more than all the other missionaries, of different Societies, five or six, together. Ten of these numerous listeners accepted the gospel, but those who did were brought in by the means of your son as well as by Mr. Edkins and the native Catechists. It frequently happens with us to hear that such a one has been converted by the preaching of such a minister or the reading of such a book, or the words of such a pious man. Never have I heard of anything of this kind in Peking, though I have been told about many individual conversions.... Was I asked the same question about Mr. Edkins, I couldn't quote one case where a Chinese confessed that his heart had been awakened by him, and yet many of them have frequently told me, in a general way, that he is a good man. Nothing more.[11]

3. DIRECTOR OF THE ANGLO-CHINESE SCHOOL

In January 1866, William Alexander Parsons Martin (1827–1916) asked Thomas to take charge of his established Anglo-Chinese School in Peking while Martin visited Kai-feng-fu (capital of Ho-nan):

10. Robert Jermain Thomas to parents, Jan. 27, 1866, Peking.
11. Pauline Morache to Robert Thomas, Oct. 26, 1867, France.

> Two days ago Dr. Martin an American missionary asked me whether I would consent to take charge of the Anglo-Chinese school attached to the Foreign Office in this city. There are but six pupils who require attendance, of two hours daily and the salary is one thousand taels per annum. I at once declined the offer, but it is my duty to report the circumstance to you. May I ask the opinion of the Board of directors? Unquestionably it is an admirable school, where a young missionary could not but progress well in his elementary Chinese studies.[12]

Thomas's demeanor showed a notable maturation compared to his previous mission fields.

First, he sought the board's approval for his opinions, a contrast to his resignation from the LMS in Shanghai and subsequent departure for Chefoo.

Second, while he had refused Muirhead's offer to take charge of the Anglo-Chinese School in Shanghai, he was willing to undertake the task in Peking.

Third, the school's annual salary of one thousand taels was equivalent to £350 in British currency,[13] whereas he had been offered £500 for the same position at the Shanghai Anglo-Chinese School.[14] This reduced financial compensation indicates that money was not his primary motivation for accepting this assignment.

At that time, there were five missionary organizations in Peking. Assisting Martin's ministry suggests Thomas aimed to promote harmony among missionaries. Martin was absent for about three months, during which Thomas assumed responsibility for the school for three months, by decision of the LMS Peking branch. In a letter Thomas sent to the LMS on April 4, 1866, he mentioned that Martin had returned from Kai-Feng-Fu.[15]

4. PREPARING FOR THE SECOND VISIT TO KOREA

Peking served as a strategically vital gateway for missions. The concentrated missionary efforts in this city held immense potential to disseminate the gospel message not only across China but also to various regions

---

12. Robert Jermain Thomas to LMS, Jan. 12, 1866, Peking.
13. Robert Jermain Thomas to parents, Feb. 4, 1864. Shanghai.
14. Robert Jermain Thomas to LMS, Jan. 31, 1865, Chefoo.
15. Robert Jermain Thomas to LMS, Apr. 4, 1866, Peking.

throughout Asia. Roland Allen, a missionary in China from 1895 to 1903, referenced Paul's missionary strategy found in Rom 15:23. Paul's mission fields were primarily administrative centers, transportation hubs, and international trade centers within the Roman Empire. Paul believed that using these strategic strongholds as bridgeheads to radiate missionary activity outwards was the most effective approach. Indeed, after completing his mission in Asia Minor, centered in cities like Corinth and Ephesus, Paul expressed a strategic desire to go to Rome to preach the gospel in Spain.[16]

Peking, as a central Asian city, was an international hub where many foreigners gathered from surrounding Asian countries. Furthermore, designated areas existed for foreign residents, and there was no structural hostility towards them. Thomas noted that missionaries found it peaceful to reside in Peking.[17] Additionally, during the Chinese New Year, embassies from across Asia visited Peking:

> The missionaries in Peking, surely one of the noblest mission fields in the Far East, cannot see with indifference the embassies which arrive once or twice a year from all parts of Asia, Koreans, Mongols and Thibetans mingle freely with us. The people of Corea, on good testimony, are more accessible to Christian truth than either of the others.[18]

Through this, foreign delegations exchanged information. In that sense, Peking was China's diplomatic hub and a central point for surrounding nations actively involved in international trade. Thomas recognized this importance. China's trade began significantly impacting the Korean economy from the mid-seventeenth century. Envoys sent to Peking during this period were called *Yeonhaengsa*. Regular missions included the Dongjihaeng (Winter Solstice Mission) and Yeokhaeng (Calendar Mission), with participants in the Dongjihaeng known as Dongjisa. The Dongjisa would arrive in Peking for the Lunar New Year, consisting of a chief envoy, a deputy envoy, an envoy secretary, and approximately thirty-five officials. However, including jaje-gungwan (young noble attendant), horse-handlers, porters, servants, and merchants, the total number reached two to three hundred. Departing Korea on the twenty-first day of the eleventh lunar month, they would arrive in Peking by the Lunar New Year.[19] Thomas reported

16. Allen, *Missionary Methods*, 18–25.
17. Robert Jermain Thomas to LMS, Apr. 4, 1866, Peking.
18. Robert Jermain Thomas to LMS, Aug. 1, 1866, Peking.
19. Guksapyeonchan Wiwonhoe, *Geosang, Jeonguk Sanggwon-eul*, 207.

the arrival of Koreans in Peking at the New Year in a letter to his parents. Thomas met with these annual Korean delegations, interacted with them, and preached the gospel:

> Peking is interesting at all times, but particularly now before the Chinese New Year. Mongols, Coreans are pouring in.[20]

> The annual Corean embassy has just departed. It has been my lot to mix more intimately with its members than any other foreigner in Peking. Some knowledge of their language and country procured me a ready admission to their official residence.[21]

In a letter to the LMS, Thomas recounted meeting a Korean man called "Pakka," and how the Bibles he had distributed along the west coast eventually reached Pyongyang, the capital of Pyongan Province:

> Curiously enough books that I had distributed on the west coast last autumn found their way to Ping-Jang the picturesque and populous provincial capital of Ping-An. A merchant named Pakka who accompanied the embassy here this winter, told me a few days since that he had obtained one of our books at Ping-Jang and had carefully perused it. He said in Corean, "Yasu Kyo chèiki mèu choosoida" = the books of the doctrine of Jesus are indeed excellent.[22]

Thomas met a Korean man along the west coast who had carefully read the Bibles he had painstakingly distributed the previous fall. The man praised the excellence of Christian doctrine. This encounter inspired Thomas to undertake a second missionary journey to Korea.

5. BACKGROUND OF THE SECOND VISIT TO KOREA

When King Cheoljong died suddenly in 1863, Gojong (1863–1907) ascended to the throne at just twelve years old. Since Gojong was so young, his father, Daewongun (1820–1898), governed the nation. Daewongun favored an isolationist policy, shutting out all foreigners. To strengthen his power, Daewongun collaborated with conservative Confucian scholars who were hostile toward Catholicism. On February 19, 1866, Catholic believer Jeon Jang-woon (1811–1866) was arrested, marking the beginning of

---

20. Robert Jermain Thomas to parents, Jan. 27, 1866, Peking.
21. Robert Jermain Thomas to LMS, Apr. 4, 1866, Peking
22. Robert Jermain Thomas to LMS, Apr. 4, 1866, Peking.

the Catholic persecution. Nine of the twelve Western priests were arrested and executed, and it's estimated that over two thousand Joseon Catholics were killed between 1866 and September 1868.[23]

Three Catholic priests—Stanislas Feron, Felix Clair Ridel, and Alphonse Nicholas Calais—managed to survive the persecution and fled to Chungcheong Province. Their representative Ridel (1830–1884) fled to Chefoo on July 7 with eleven other Catholics.[24] Ridel met with French General Pierre-Gustave Rose (1812–1883) in Tientsin, reported the brutal massacre in Joseon, and requested the rescue of the two remaining French priests. Ridel then returned to Chefoo and awaited Rose's next move.[25]

Admiral Rose immediately informed M. de Bellonet, the French Chargé d'Affaires in Peking, about the incident. De Bellonet decided to organize a French expedition to Joseon. While preparations for the expedition were underway, Thomas received a request to serve as an interpreter for the French fleet:

> The French ambassador has requested me to accompany the Admiral, and I am the only foreigner living who is acquainted with the coast and who has a *general* acquaintance with the language.[26]

Why was Thomas, a Protestant missionary, chosen as the interpreter for the French fleet? The reason can be found in Edkins's letter:

> The French Admiral will probably ask Thomas to go as interpreter. He has no interpreter except a refugee missionary, who having lived in extreme quietude hidden among the converts, is not likely to have the local knowledge which Thomas acquired during his three months on the Coast. Besides, we are told at the French Legation that the Admiral does not trust the French clergy and as it is supposed that they are viewed by the Coreans as political intriguers, the Admiral would be glad to have as an interpreter a person not belonging to the French clergy.[27]

First, Edkins wrote that the French priests lacked knowledge of Joseon because they lived in seclusion with their converts. This contrasted sharply with Thomas, who had traveled along the west coast for two and

---

23. Dallet, *Histoire de l'Eglise en Coree*, 480.
24. Griffis, *Corea, the Hermit Nation*, 376.
25. Griffis, *Corea, the Hermit Nation*, 483.
26. Robert Jermain Thomas to LMS, Aug. 1, 1866, Peking. Thomas's italics.
27. Joseph Edkins to LMS, July 25, 1866, Peking.

a half months. Second, Admiral Rose didn't trust the French clergy. Third, Admiral Rose didn't want to worsen political tensions by bringing Catholic French clergy with him, so he requested a Protestant missionary. According to Morache, Thomas was chosen as the interpreter for the French fleet on the recommendation of M. Lemaine from the French Legation in Peking:

> I knew by M. Lemaine, our French interpreter, that M. de Bellonet was very happy to secure Mr. Thomas and that he wished to settle immediately the pecuniary appointment.[28]

Thomas was the only Westerner in Peking who had experience visiting Joseon. He was widely recognized among Westerners for his foreign language skills, especially his fluent French. Thomas spoke French well[29] and could preach in Chinese. Although Thomas wasn't fluent in Korean, he could speak and write the Chinese used by the Joseon upper class. This is why France considered Thomas a suitable interpreter.

6. MOTIVATION OF THE SECOND VISIT TO KOREA

Thomas's motivation in visiting Korea was to evangelize to Koreans, master the language, and lay the groundwork for Christian mission.

> Mr. Thomas objected that this was the missionary establishment's business, not his; he also refused any advance of money for the voyage expenses—Mr. Edkins joined a young native skilled in map-drawing.[30]

Two years after Thomas's death in Korea, the Congregational denomination to which Thomas belonged issued its *Congregational Year Book*:

> The fact is, he wanted to go to Corea by some means in order to perfect his knowledge in the language, so as to be able to translate the scriptures in that language, and establish a Protestant mission in that dark land.[31]

Thomas's activities in Korea also offer significant insights into his motivations. He distributed Bibles and Christian books to people whenever he

---

28. Pauline Morache to Robert Thomas, Oct. 26, 1867, France.
29. Robert Jermain Thomas to LMS, Mar. 8, 1861, London.
30. Pauline Morache to Robert Thomas, Oct. 26, 1867, France.
31. *Congregational Year Book 1868*, 298.

had the opportunity. In his last letter to the LMS, Thomas reported that one of Dongjisa had requested the Gospel of Matthew the previous January:

> Religious books were distributed by me last year all along the west coast. In January of the year a note in Chinese was put into my hand by a member of the Corean Embassy in Peking begging a copy of Matthew gospel, like that a foreigner had distributed on the coast of Corea. These facts speak for themselves. It does not dissipate our force to extend the influence of the Word of God.[32]

It's clear Thomas went to Korea to evangelize to Koreans, and Edkins fully agreed. The previous chapter showed Thomas and Edkins working together harmoniously in Peking. The LMS had committees in three locations in China: the North China Committee, the South China Committee, and the Central China Committee. Peking fell under the jurisdiction of the North China Committee, where Edkins was the leader. Morache's letter clearly reveals the discussions in Peking regarding Thomas's visit to Korea:

> The missionaries in Peking, of five different boards, have established a rule according to which they decide by vote or persuasion, every important question. In this occurrence, Mr. Edkins told me there were two against. One, an American by political antipathy, the other, Mr. Edkins said, because it was for a Roman Catholic interest. . . . "We have another meeting to-night and I think we'll bring the two opponents round" so they did.[33]

In Peking, five different missionary societies collaborated for their mission activities: the LMS, the American Board of Commissioners for Foreign Missions (ABCFM), the Presbyterian Church in the USA (Northern) Board of Foreign Missions, the Church Missionary Society (CMS), and the Protestant Episcopal Church Mission. Those carrying out missionary work in Peking established local boards for each organization and agreed to thoroughly discuss all matters. These five missionary societies convened two meetings to discuss Thomas's visit to Korea. It appears Edkins chaired these meetings, likely because Thomas was an LMS missionary and his Korea visit was the main agenda. As Edkins was the leader, Thomas wouldn't have been able to visit Korea without his consent. Despite two initial objections,

---

32. Robert Jermain Thomas to LMS, Aug. 1, 1866, Peking.
33. Pauline Morache to Robert Thomas, Oct. 26, 1867, France.

the board seems to have approved Thomas's visit to Korea. These objections, as seen in Morache's letter, were resolved in the second meeting.[34]

Further evidence of Edkins's full agreement with Thomas's visit to Korea is that Edkins arranged for a Chinese colleague to accompany Thomas to assist him:

> I send with him a young Chinese student who will be useful in affording Christian instruction throughout the journey to those willing to receive it.[35]

For Thomas's second visit to Korea, Cho Nung-bong, a Chinese man from Peking, consistently accompanied him and remained with Thomas until the end in Korea. Edkins decided to send Cho Nung-bong to help make Thomas's visit more successful.

7. ITINERARY FROM PEKING TO CHEFOO

Around July 18, Thomas departed Peking for Tientsin.[36] After arriving in Tientsin, while waiting for a ship to Chefoo, he received a letter from M. de Bellonet:

> On arriving at Tientsin, I was told by the French consul that a little insurrection having taken place in Saigon, the Admiral had left Chefoo for Hong Kong, but would probably return in a month. I resolved to proceed to Chefoo not wishing to pass any time idly here.[37]

Subsequently, Thomas traveled to Chefoo and met Ridel, who provided him with a detailed account of the Catholic persecution in Korea. Upon hearing the news, he sought a way to go to Korea.

The *General Sherman*, owned by an American named Mr. Preston, was set to enter Tientsin harbor in mid-July and would contact Messrs. Meadows & Co. to arrange trade with Korea. Hogarth, an employee of Messrs. Meadows & Co., knew Thomas from Chefoo and was preparing for trade in Korea. Morache recalled his last meeting with Thomas as follows:

---

34. Pauline Morache to Robert Thomas, Oct. 26, 1867, France.
35. Josept Edkins to LMS, July 25, 1866, Peking.
36. Josept Edkins to LMS, July 25, 1866, Peking.
37. Robert Jermain Thomas to LMS, Aug. 1, 1866, Peking.

> A fortnight after this, your son called and told me that he was going to Corea without waiting for Admiral Rose who was certain to come and would be glad to find his way prepared by such enquiries as Mr. Thomas could get. "You'll excuse me if I don't tell you by what ship I am sailing." This was said very politely but in that decided tone which admits no gainsaying. Alas! I never saw him again.[38]

According to this letter, Thomas proceeded to Pyongyang without waiting for Admiral Rose's return, even though he knew Rose was coming back. After Thomas completed his first visit to Korea and returned to Peking, an LMS magazine sent to its supporters featured an article titled "Visit of the Revd Thomas to Corea" along with Thomas's long letter to the LMS. This article deeply impressed supporters and helped them understand the mission in China.

> Our brother had no sooner arrived in the north, whither he proceeded by instruction of the Directors, than, in connection with the Rev. A. Williamson, he resolved to proceed, pro tem., as a distributor of Scriptures, to the west coast of Corea, a country utterly unknown to any but Catholic missionaries. It was an enterprise undertaken not without considerable uncertainty and peril; but we are thankful that our devoted brethren, after travelling for four months amidst perils by water and perils by land, returned to their starting-point in safety.[39]

The LMS's response to Thomas's first visit to Korea was positive, and it influenced Thomas's second visit to Korea:

> On arriving at Tientsin, I was told by the French consul that a little insurrection having taken place in Saigon, the Admiral had left Chefoo for Hong Kong, but would probably return in a month. I resolved to proceed to Chefoo not wishing to pass any time idly here. Trusting the directors will approve of our efforts to spread the doctrines of the Bible unmixed with human error, in this unknown land.[40]

Thomas set out on his second missionary journey to Korea, confident that the LMS would appreciate his efforts and affirm his commitment.

---

38. Pauline Morache to Robert Thomas, Oct. 26, 1867, France.
39. London Missionary Society, "Visit of the R. J. Thomas," July 2, 1866, 200.
40. Robert Jermain Thomas to LMS, Aug. 1, 1866, Peking.

London Mission, Chefoo,
August 1, 1866

My dear Dr. Tidman,

Whilst we are startled with the news of war in Europe, countries nearer at hand, well nigh ignored at home, are occupying our attention. A foul and wicked massacre has recently taken place in Corea.

Two Roman Catholic Bishops and seven missionaries have been barbarously tortured and then beheaded. For many years these devoted agents of the Papacy have hidden themselves in that almost unknown and strictly watched kingdom.

A little over a month ago a Native Corean junk was seen entering the harbour with a French Tricolour at its fore mast. It brought the French missionary Father Ridel and a crew of Coreans all, save two, Christians. According to Father Ridel's account this massacre was caused by the ominous advance of Russian power on the North East frontier of Corea. Other accounts assert that the Catholics were plotting secretly the overthrow of the government. It is certain the nominal adherents of Catholicism in Corea amount to some thousands. At the capital Wang-Ching, the Bishop had established a college, set up a printing press for native books, had spent many years in compiling a Chinese-Corean Latin Dictionary and works bearing on the history, resources and geography of Corea. All these, so Father Ridel tells me, have been burned and also all the missals, catechisms etc. already used for years composed in the colloquial of the country and elegantly printed in the native character. Last year when in Korea I procured a complete set of these latter works, which will be of great use in the ultimate compiling of purer elementary Christian works.

When the sad news of the wholesale murder of these missionaries reached us in Peking, the French ambassador immediately resolved, in concert with the French Admiral, who had just left the Capital for Tientsin, to send an expedition immediately to rescue two missionaries who are supposed to be living amongst the Corean mountains, to demand satisfaction for the massacre, and to open Corea, closed for so many hundred years, to the commerce of the West.

The missionaries in Peking, surely one of the noblest mission fields in the Far East, cannot see with indifference the embassies which arrive once or twice a year from all parts of Asia, Coreans, Mongols and Thibetans mingle freely with us. The people of Corea, on good testimony, are more accessible to Christian truth than either of the others. Buddhism is weaker in Corea than in China. The Chinese character is understood better in all parts of Corea by the lower classes than in the north of China. Religious books were distributed by me last year all along the West coast. In January of this year a note in Chinese was put into my hand by a member of the Corean Embassy in Peking begging a copy of the Matthew Gospel, like that a foreigner had distributed on the coast of Corea. These facts speak for themselves. It does not dissipate our force to extend the influence of the Word of God. In my spare hours I have diligently kept up my acquaintance with the Corean vernacular. Little did I think that, last year tempest tossed along a dangerous and inhospitable shore, I should have the honour of being the first Protestant missionary to visit Corea. The French Ambassador has requested me to accompany the Admiral, and I am the only foreigner living who is acquainted with the coast and who has a general acquaintance with the language. Mr. Edkins fully and entirely agreed with me that it was better to leave immediately for Chefoo. On arriving at Tientsin, I was told by the French Consul that a little insurrection having taken place in Saigon, the Admiral had left Chefoo for Hong Kong, but would probably return in a month. I resolved to proceed to Chefoo not wishing to pass any time idly here, I have accepted a passage over to Corea, in the schooner of a friendly English merchant. I take a good supply of books with me and am quite sanguine that I shall be welcomed by the people. I hope to meet the Admiral's frigate on the Corean coast.

Our work is progressing so fast, under God's blessing in Peking that I was very loth to leave it for even a few weeks. But the representations of Mr. Edkins and all the other missionaries, of the importance of a Protestant Missionary presenting himself in the country at once, led me to take a step which may subsequently exercise a most beneficial reflex action on our mission in the Capital. Trusting the Directors will approve of our efforts to spread the doctrines of the Bible unmixed with human error, in this unknown land.

Believe me, dear Dr. Tidman,
Very sincerely yours,
R. Jermain Thomas

Robert Jermain Thomas the 2nd Trip in Korea

Chapter 6

The Second Visit to Korea

IN PEKING, ENCOUNTERS WITH Koreans sparked Thomas's missionary interest in the country, which then transformed into a fervent passion during his first visit. With even greater aspirations than before, he embarked on his second voyage to a Korea that was now somewhat familiar. Like the rest of the *General Sherman* crew, Thomas had no idea of the fate awaiting him—he would become the first Protestant martyr to open the door for missions in Korea.

1. SOURCES

Much of the research on Thomas has focused on the *General Sherman* incident. As a result, Thomas's life and character in Korea are often regarded as fully confirmed. However, a close examination of the literature reveals errors and inconsistencies in detailed accounts of his death. These discrepancies have led to divergent analyses and evaluations among researchers studying the incident. Many of the errors stem from inconsistent use of sources and varying standards of reliability. In this book, information related to the *General Sherman* incident will be examined using three types of sources: American diplomatic documents, Christian literature, and Korean records of the incident.

1) American Diplomatic Documents

American diplomatic documents concerning the *General Sherman* incident were compiled months after the event. Captain R. W. Shufeldt (1822–1895) of the USS *Wachusett*, dispatched by the US government to investigate the incident, departed Chefoo on January 22, 1867. He brought along American missionary Hunter Corbett (1835–1920) as an interpreter and Yu Won-tae as a pilot for the voyage to Korea's west coast.[1] The documentation includes information Shufeldt collected during his stay in Korea, as well as data gathered by Commander John C. Febiger (1821–1898) of the USS *Shenandoah*. Febiger left Chefoo on May 18, 1867, and spent forty days on the Korean coast to investigate rumors of two surviving Westerners. Their sources of information and testimony included: 1) French priests who escaped the 1866 persecution, 2) French soldiers who invaded Korea in 1866, 3) Chinese pilot Wu Wen Tai, who accompanied Thomas on his first visit to Korea, 3) Messrs. Meadows & Co., owners of the *General Sherman*.

2) Christian Literature

The earliest Christian literary information comes from records of missionaries in Korea, including James S. Gale (1863–1937),[2] who served there from 1888 to 1936. Oh Mun-hwan (1903–1962) also collected testimonies and published the first book about Thomas. Additionally, there are accounts from Koreans—especially Christians—who witnessed the incident. However, these testimonies have limitations, as they were collected decades after the event and rely on the recollections of elderly individuals reportedly present during the *General Sherman* incident.[3]

---

    1. "Library of Congress, Microfilms, Roll 28299. *Abstract Log the* USS *Wachusett.* R. W. Shufeldt Esq. 23 January 1865–1868 (This Document is hereafter cited as *Log of Wachusett*), 22 January 1867," cited in Kim, *Kundae Hanmi Kwangea-sa*, 214.

    2. Gale, "Fate of the *General Sherman*," 252–54.

    3. Below is the nature of main sources cited so far in studies on Thomas.

Source	Content and Characteristics	Limitation and Note

3) Korean Government Records

Research into Korean government records focuses on information provided by frontline officials who directly experienced the *General Sherman* incident. A crucial primary source is the *Jang-kea* (Record of the Pyengan Army Camp), a report submitted to the central government by Pyeongan Governor Pak Kyu-su. In the Joseon Dynasty, a *Jang-kea* was a document submitted by an official dispatched to an outer province to report important matters under their jurisdiction directly to the king. This *Jang-kea* covers the period from the *General Sherman*'s arrival in Korea until the conclusion of the incident. It was written in nineteenth-century Classical Chinese, and the entire *Jang-kea* has not been translated into Korean. For

Paegang Record	High historical value record by Lee Heung-geun, son of Lee Hyun-ik, for Central army, who was detained in the *General Sherman*. Especially, it alone says that Chosön planned to exterminate the *General Sherman* well before Lee Hyun-ik was kidnapped.	Because the original copy and text has not been released and Kim Yang-sun's *A Study on Korean History of Christianity* does not indicate the extent to which it was based on this source, care should be taken in using it.
Journal of Pyengyang	Organized in detail by date, this source alone mentions the process of praying to mountain gods, or using fire attack to repulse the *General Sherman* by Pyengyang military and people, and the scenes of Thomas's landing and meeting Chosön officials several days before the *General Sherman* was set to fire.	Original copy is inaccessible. As often seen from journals of Gun or Eup, errors may occur in the course of compiling what has been transmitted by word of mouth.
Gojong Chronicles	Official record by the government with detailed arrangement of subject by day and time. Especially, it includes many specific references to the *General Sherman* and Thomas.	When reported from province to the center, the content might have been distorted to the advantage of Chosön and themselves.
Testimony collected by Oh Munhwan	Abundant in imaginative stories not found in records. Only this testimony covers Thomas's propagation activities, the last scene of the *General Sherman* and Thomas, stories about people involved in this incident and converted later, etc.	There can be inaccurate information with elapse of time and also a possibility for exaggeration or embellishment because most of the witnesses are Christians.

this study, the author translated *Jang-kea*, which consists of approximately 8,400 characters.

Pak Kyu-su, who authored *Jang-kea*, was the Pyeongan provincial governor and the highest-ranking Joseon government official who commanded the *General Sherman* incident. Excerpts from the *Jang-kea* are also recorded in *Journal of Korean Government Secret Service*, *Gojong Taehwangje Sillok* (Veritable records of Emperor Gojong), and *Ilseongnok* (Diary of self-reflection). Park Yong-kyu, who meticulously studied many documents related to the *General Sherman* incident, including *Gojong Taehwangje Sillok*, pointed out, "Upon examining domestic historical records, I found that the descriptions of the *General Sherman* lacked consistency and uniformity. They also contain many errors that do not align with the facts."[4] These errors arose because records from various government departments either summarized Pak Kyu-su's *Jang-kea* or selectively recorded only necessary parts. Additionally, discrepancies in dates are due to the time it took for the *Jang-kea* to be transmitted from Pyongyang to Hanyang, and each document recorded information based on the date it was received.

All Joseon government records, including *Jang-kea*, have the following limitations:

First, the *General Sherman* violated Joseon law by entering an inland river and committed illegal acts, making it a clear act of provocation against another nation. Therefore, the records inevitably portrayed the *General Sherman* in a hostile light.[5] In government records, the *General Sherman* was referred to as a "Western monster" or "Western enemy," which led to records about Thomas also being left from a negative perspective.

Second, the *General Sherman* not only entered Korea illegally but also instigated acts of violence. The initial confrontation began with the kidnapping of Commander Lee Hyun-ik, which led the officials and citizens of Pyongyang to fire stones, arrows, and firearms, sparking a skirmish. In response, the *General Sherman* began its own attack, firing cannons.

Third, there were no survivors from the *General Sherman*. Consequently, no records or information exist that could represent the *General Sherman*'s perspective.

---

4. Park, "Robert J. Thomas Seongyosa," 35.
5. Griffis, *Corea, the Hermit Nation*, 395.

2. MISSION WORK

During his first visit to Korea, Thomas primarily operated in coastal and island areas; however, for his second visit, he sought to work inland.

1) Bible Distribution

According to *Jang-kea*, there are records of contact between Thomas and local residents. To obtain information unavailable through official government channels, Pak Kyu-su disguised government officials as tourists and sent them aboard the *General Sherman* on the afternoon of August 18. They reported on the ship's internal structure and delivered written records of their conversations to Pak Kyu-su.[6] This suggests Koreans were able to board the *General Sherman* quite naturally. Additionally, *Pyongyang-gi* (Pyongyang diary) records that Thomas distributed New Testaments and books to everyone he met.[7] Testimony from Hong Sin-gil regarding the Jangsa Port incident also remains:

> On August 20, the schooner went up a little farther, to a place called Jangsa Port. A very interesting event took place at this place. It happened to be market day at Taipyung nearby. A boy named Hong Shin-kil, who had been at the Market, heard the news of the coming of a foreign vessel. He went home and persuaded two other boys to go with him to the foreign boat in a boat rowed by them. Mr. Thomas, who was looking out for Koreans, was very glad to see them. They were received by him on deck and taken to his room. There were many book-cases there, the boys were given some cakes first, and then a few copies of books. Mr. Hong says that there he saw potatoes for the first time in his life. After two or three hours they came back home with the books.[8]

According to Choi Ik-ro, the situation at Dumujin, Baengnyeongdo, where the *General Sherman* stopped on its way to Pyongyang, was as follows:

> When the foreign vessel came here, I went out with other friends to see it. One of the foreigners was very kind, and we were entertained by him. We did not know what kind of food he was giving

---

6. Pak, *Jang-kea*, Aug. 19, 1866.
7. Kim, *Chogi Hanmi Gwangyeui Jaejomyeong*, 41.
8. Oh, "Two Visits," 116.

The Second Visit to Korea

us at that time, but I know now that it was cakes. I also received some books from him but later on owing to the threatening attitude of the soldiers we had to throw them away or give them up. The Mandarin ordered all the books the foreigner had distributed to be taken to his office on three bull-carts (rather small ones on this island), and later sent all of them to the Ongchin Naval Office.[9]

Thomas showed a consistent pattern when meeting Koreans not affiliated with the government. He would welcome them, bring them to his room for more serious conversations, and build relationships. Thomas socialized with the Koreans, shared cake with them, and then distributed Christian books. This pattern was consistent with his previous activities interacting with Chinese people in Shanghai.

2) Onshore Ministry

The Korean government officials responsible for the investigation visited the *General Sherman* six times: five from Hwanghae Province, one from Pyeongan Province, plus an additional unofficial inspection. On August 19, a Korean official disguised as a civilian boarded the *General Sherman* for an unofficial inquiry—Thomas was not aboard at that time. The officials spoke with Cho Nung-bong and later included their conversation in their report.[10] So, where was Thomas when the ship was anchored?

On August 24, three foreigners, including Thomas, went ashore at Jangsa Port and climbed up to the Mangyeong-dae Gazebo. They surveyed the surroundings, visited Okhyeon, and then returned to the ship.[11] A North Korean history publication, *Chosön Chönsa* (A Comprehensive History of Korea), asserts that "Thomas and two other foreigners illegally entered Okhyeon for reconnaissance. They also assaulted Korean females,"[12] but no such claims appear in the official Korean government records.

On August 26, the *General Sherman* arrived at Hansa Gazebo, where four foreigners, including Thomas, disembarked and spent several hours on land. However, the investigators reported that they did not know what

---

9. Oh, "Two Visits," 114.
10. Pak, *Jang-kea*, Aug. 19, 1866.
11. Pak, *Jang-kea*, Aug. 24, 1866.
12. Kwahak Paekkwa Chulpan-sa, *Chosön Chönsa*, 72.

Thomas did while ashore.¹³ Additionally, *Pyongyang-gi* notes that Thomas distributed New Testaments and other books to everyone he encountered.¹⁴

According to researcher Oh Mun-hwan, at Seokho-jeong Gazebo, located between Jangsa Port and the Mangyeong-dae Gazebo, "many Koreans gathered to see the foreigners":

> Here also Mr. Thomas distributed many books. A young man in the crowd named Kim Young-sup received one of the books distributed by Mr. Thomas. The title of that book was Easy Introduction to the Truth. He took it home and kept it secretly in his book box, reading it stealthily from time to time. He at last got to know the truth of Christianity from this book, taught it to his son Kim Chong-kwon and his nephew Kim Sung-chip, both of whom later on became elders of the Presbyterian Church.¹⁵

Table 1. The Testimonies Collected by Oh Moon-hwan

The Testifiers	Ages of Testifiers	Testimony	Christian or Not
Ji Dal-hae (son Ji Taek-joo testified)	53	Visited the *General Sherman* and received Bible. Read Bible in the family. Arrested and executed.	
Hong Shin-gil	19	Visited the *General Sherman* with 2–3 friends on boat. Read Bible.	Later became Christian and established Hari church
		"At the time, too many people were on board the ship and the ship was in danger by overweight. The *General Sherman* gave more than 500 Bibles at Pori Port."¹⁶	
Kim Yeong-seop		Received Bible (date not known)	His son Kim Jong-gwon worked at Daesong-ri church

13. Pak, *Jang-kea*, Aug. 26, 1866.

14. Kim, *Chogi Hanmi Gwangyeui Jaejomyeong*, 41.

15. Oh, "Two Visits," 119.

16. Hong Shin-gil's testimony cited in Han, "General Sherman Sagunkwa Thomas Sunkyomoonje," 16n18.

Choi Chi-ryang	11	Got one Bible when the *General Sherman* was burnt	Elder at Oebyeol-chon church
Lee Shin-haeng	20s	Same as above	The first female Protestant Christian
Hwang Myeong-dae	20s	Hwang said, "A person threw Bibles at the bow when the *General Sherman* was burning, while shouting Jesus."	Attended Jowan-gri church
Han Seok-jin, who collected the oral statements of survivors		A person threw Bibles at the bow when the *General Sherman* was burning.	
Samuel A. Moffett		"I saw substantial number of people carrying Bibles received from Thomas when establishing a church in Pyengyang."	

3) Explaining the Differences with Catholicism

Thomas tried to explain in Korea that Protestantism differed from Catholicism. When Kim Nak-soo and Jo Won-gook visited the *General Sherman* as inquiry officers on August 21, Thomas stated,

> Why does your country expel Catholicism? Our Protestantism, imitating the way of heaven, can rectify people's minds, change wicked customs, and make people good by possessing all of humanity, righteousness, loyalty, and filial piety, so it is different from Catholicism.[17]

His explanation continued:

> We Protestants are different from Catholics. We correct the minds of people by truth and enlighten evil habits. We teach people on filial piety, mercy, justice and loyalty. We make good people.[18]

The *General Sherman* arrived at Jooyeong Port, located at the mouth of the Daedong River, on August 16. Kim Yeong-seop received books

---

17. Pak, *Jang-kea*, Aug. 22, 1866.
18. Pak, *Jang-kea*, Aug. 22, 1866.

from Thomas at Mangyeongjeong on August 24. A standoff between the *General Sherman* and the Korean government began when military officer Lee Hyun-ik was kidnapped. Thus, during those ten days inland in Korea, Thomas seized every opportunity and did everything he could to advance his mission.

3. INTERACTION WITH KOREAN OFFICIALS

Thomas, who arrived in Korea aboard the *General Sherman*, met with Korean officials and explained the mission and purpose of the ship's visit. Although their official and brief interaction was far from sufficient for true mutual understanding, their exchanges are recorded in multiple historical sources. In this section, we review those materials to dispel misunderstandings and factual distortions about Thomas, correcting misconceptions and presenting a clearer, more accurate perspective.

1) Was Thomas the Captain of the *General Sherman*?

When John C. Febriger came to Korea to investigate the *General Sherman*, the Korean government told him, "Thomas came on a foreign schooner illegally invading our country."[19] This suggests that Thomas's influence on the *General Sherman* was very significant. A report from Jeong Dae-shik on August 16 states, "Thomas directs everything on the ship,"[20] and on August 18, Yoo Cho-hwan recorded that "Thomas is the leader of the foreigners."[21] Han Gyoo-moo wrote that Thomas was not just a simple interpreter but an important figure who could determine the ship's navigation policy. Consequently, Han Gyoo-moo held Thomas responsible for the *General Sherman*'s misfortune on the Daedong River.[22]

Thomas spoke some Korean and was fluent in Chinese. Therefore, it is highly likely that he played a crucial role in most of the interactions with the Koreans. For this reason, the Koreans may have exaggerated Thomas's importance and perceived him as the captain of the *General Sherman*. Wu

---

19. Febiger Letters, "B." Sam Hoa, District Magistrate, Le to the Honorable American. Mou Chin, Third Month, Twenty-fifth, in Kim, *Kundae Hanmi Kwangea-sa*, 241.

20. *Gojong Taehwangje Sillok*, Aug. 24, 1866.

21. Pak, *Jang-kea*, Aug. 8, 1866.

22. Han Kyu-moo, "*General Sherman* Sagunkwa Thomas Sunkyomoonje," 15.

Wen Tai's testimony regarding this can be found in a letter from Messrs. Meadows & Co. to British consul Mongan.

> He (Wu Wen Tai) is 43 years of age, and has traded for many years with Corea. "Mr. Thomas constantly wanted to land and ramble about, but the pilot advised him against doing so." Thomas wished to keep the pilot and let his junk return to Shantung, but his junkmen would not hear of it, saying they could not face his family without him. On the pilot reaching the mouth of the Ping Yang River he had some conversation with the Coreans there, and they told him that their Sovereign would by no means trade with foreigners. My teacher (Thomas) acted as Interpreter during the above conversation, which lasted a good time.[23]

We can draw the following conclusions from the records above.

First, Thomas's activities were restricted during the initial visit to Korea. He wasn't even allowed to leave the ship for a walk. Second, Thomas wanted to return to Shantung. He learned about Korea's perilous situation from the officials in charge of the investigation and considered a visit to Pyengyang too dangerous. However, the pilots refused to turn back. Third, Thomas's role on the *General Sherman* was merely that of an interpreter. The Koreans Wu Wen Tai saw were Lee Gil-ho and Shin Bong-jin, who had visited the *General Sherman* at the mouth of the Daedong River. Lee Gil-ho and Shin Bong-jin reported that Lee Pal-haeng made the decisions and Thomas translated his words. In other words, Thomas was Lee Pal-haeng's interpreter.[24] Another record states that Lee Pal-haeng was the owner of the *General Sherman*.[25] However, the ship's owner was Preston, and Thomas was his interpreter. Yet another Korean record says that Thomas wanted to leave Korea. Between three and five o'clock in the afternoon on August 23, Lee Hyun-ik and Shin Tae-jeong boarded the *General Sherman* and had the following conversation:

> Lee Hyun-ik and Shin Tae-jeong: You keep going up the river, not going away. We have to talk.
>
> The General Sherman (no person's name): We will go away after we trade our goods for Korean goods.

---

23. Extract from Mr. Mackey's letter to Messrs. Meadows & Co., Oct. 8, 1866, Chefoo.
24. *Gojong Taehwangje Sillok*, Aug. 24, 1866.
25. Pak, *Jang-kea*, Aug. 22, 1866. Lee Pal-haeng said he was the owner of the ship and he was from Denmark. In addition, there were three Americans and two British. Among them, Wilson was a naturalized American from Denmark.

> Lee Hyun-ik and Shin Tae-jeong: Trade with foreign countries is prohibited in Korea. Our government needs to talk with China. We can help you if your ship has difficulty or provide you with some supplies; however, we cannot do trading at our will.
>
> When we spoke like this, Thomas (a westerner) and Jo Neung-bong (a Chinese) listened carefully. It seemed they were going to comply with our request. However, the ship owner (Preston) and the cargo owner (Hogarth) insisted on trading.[26]

According to this report, Thomas did not have the authority to make final decisions. Therefore, he was not the captain of the *General Sherman*.

2) Was the Attack Ordered by the King?

Given that Korea was under a strong royal authority, it was definitively assumed that the *General Sherman* was burned by the king's command. A letter from Messrs. Meadows & Co. records the testimony of French Admiral Rose:

> The French Admiral's account is that when the General Sherman appeared at Ping Yang, the father of the king of Corea asked what was to be done with her, and the king replied, let her be burnt with all on board of her; and that this was executed accordingly.[27]

In his thesis, Goh Moo-song argued that Pak Kyu-su reported the situation to the king and requested royal approval to burn the ship and kill everyone on board. Goh Moo-song stated that on September 4, 1866, the king issued such a command.[28] According to this record, the *General Sherman* was burned by the king's order. However, a Korean government document records the following conversation between King Gojong, Lee Gyeong-jae (1800–1873), Kim Byeong-hak (1821–1879), and Jo Doo-soon (1796–1870) on September 4:

> Lee Gyeong-jae: Foreign ships have the right to navigate along Korean "sea." However, they did not come into the Korean "river" before. The foreign ship that came to Ganghwa Island had left. But this ship that came to Pyengyang does not go away. It gives us concern and surprise.

---

26. Pak, *Jang-kea*, Aug. 24, 1866.
27. Oh, "Two Visits," 113.
28. Goh, "Western and Asian Portrayals," 151.

The Second Visit to Korea

Go-jong (the king): Right. Foreigners can navigate our sea but they should not come into our river and our land.

Kim Byeong-hak: This incident is the first one of that kind.

Go-jong (the king): It is because we had been too generous to western ships.

Jo Doo-soon: Your majesty is right.

Go-jong (the king): I want strict instruction to the whole country to be alarmed for the cowardly foreigners.

Kim Byeong-hak: We should be harsher towards the foreigners. We have to have a close investigation. It is essential to maintain the foundation and continuity of the country. If we allow such evil people to go around in our country, we are not a civilized country. We should resolve this crisis strictly by law.

Jo Doo-soon: I agree with Kim Byeong-hak. We should resolve this crisis strictly by law.

Kim Byeong-hak: Your majesty. This is an important subject. I suggest we meet again tomorrow and talk about it for a decision.

Go-jong (the king): We will do that.[29]

The *General Sherman* was burned and its crew was killed in Pyongyang on September 2,[30] before the meeting with King Gojong on September 4, 1866. Pak Kyu-su never requested the king's approval for the *General Sherman* incident. A record from the Pyongan-do Military Camp, dated September 10, explicitly states that the *General Sherman* was not burned by the king's command:

> This foreign ship came into our country but we could not stop it. The ship came up to Pyengyang castle but again we could not let it go away. They threatened us; they kidnapped Lee Hyun-ik and insulted him. The incident is at last closed by their death. We could not abide by the merciful intention of the king to persuade the foreigners and let them go away without violence. As a government officer, I admit I am guilty and I am sorry.[31]

The destruction of the *General Sherman* and the deaths of its crew did not occur under direct royal command. Instead, Pak Kyu-su made that

---

29. Lee, *Hanmi Kwangea yengu-sa*, 81–82.
30. London Missionary Society, "Annual Report of the LMS for 1867," 80.
31. Pak, *Jang-kea*, Sept. 9, 1866.

decision amid the chaos unfolding in Pyongyang, choosing to burn the ship to restore order and protect the city.

3) Did the *General Sherman* Go to Pyongyang at Thomas's Request?

According to *Journal of Pyongyang*, Cho Nung-bong stated that the *General Sherman* was sailing south for trade. However, when Thomas arrived in Peking on August 9, he told Preston and Hogarth that they could make a large profit by going to Korea. Thomas also mentioned that he had a letter from the Chinese government in Peking to the Korean government. The *General Sherman* then set off for Pyongyang.[32] This raises the question: did the *General Sherman* go to Pyongyang based on Thomas's suggestion? To answer this, we need to examine the following points.

First, on June 24, the *Surprise*, a ship captained by McCaslin, was wrecked on Korea's west coast. Captain McCaslin and his seven crew members were treated well by the Korean government and handed over to the American consul in Youngku, China, Francis P. Knight. McCaslin later met with the *General Sherman*'s owner, Preston, in Shanghai, who told him that the *General Sherman* would be going to Korea and sailing up the Daedong River.[33]

Second, a letter dated December 27, 1866, from Shufeldt, the captain of the USS *Wachusett*, records that Preston had expressed a desire to explore the Daedong River when he was making a contract with the British company Messrs. Meadows & Co.[34]

Third, a letter from Messrs. Meadows & Co. to the British consul contains the following:

> About three months back the American schooner the General Sherman arrived at this port, and the owner, Mr. Preston, who had come on board the vessel, consigned her to our care. After we had discharged her inward cargo, which was sent to our care, Mr. Preston, who resided on shore in our house soon after his arrival, and during his stay in Tientsin, we came to the determination to see if any business could be done in a venture to Corea; we

---

32. Kim, *Chogi hanmi kwangae Jeajomyung*, 33.
33. Kim, *Kundae Hanmi Kwangea-sa*, 214.
34. Kim, *Kundae Hanmi Kwangea-sa*, 215.

The Second Visit to Korea

consequently loaded the vessel and dispatched her on a trading voyage to Corea.[35]

Therefore, Preston, the owner of the *General Sherman*, had already prepared for a trading voyage to Pyongyang. He had signed a contract with Messrs. Meadows & Co. for the trip and came to Chefoo to embark. Thomas had no influence on the *General Sherman*'s journey to Pyongyang. According to Cho Nung-bong, Thomas arrived in Peking on August 9, which was the very day the *General Sherman* departed from Chefoo for Korea.

4. CONTROVERSIES SURROUNDING THE *GENERAL SHERMAN* AND THOMAS

Despite the limitations of available sources, research related to Thomas continues steadily. In this book, I will exclude areas regarding the *General Sherman* incident and Thomas that are already well-established and agreed upon. Instead, I will focus on topics that require correction or reevaluation.

1) Was the *General Sherman* Originally the *Princess Royal*?

Until now, research on the *General Sherman* in Christian literature,[36] studies of Korean-American relations,[37] and North Korean history[38] have consistently asserted that it was a renamed American warship, the *Princess Royal*. Apart from Kim Myeong-ho, who first raised this issue online in 2005, no scholars had suggested that the *General Sherman* might have been a different vessel. According to official US documents, the *Princess Royal*, which came to be known as the *General Sherman*, was used as a US warship, decommissioned in 1865, converted into a merchant ship in 1885, and renamed the *General Sherman* before it sank in 1874.[39]

---

35. Messrs. Meadows & Co. to Mr. Mongan, Consul, Oct. 23, 1866, Tientsin.

36. Kim Sung-tea, "General Sherman Sagune," 136. This article labels the picture of the *Princess Royal* as that of the *General Sherman*.

37. Kim, *Kundae Hanmi Kwangea-sa*. The picture of the *Princess Royal* is also regarded as the *General Sherman* in this book.

38. In 2006, North Korea issued stamps commemorating the 140th anniversary of the *General Sherman* victory. The stamp shows the *General Sherman* on fire, but the picture is that of the *Princess Royal*.

39. Kim, *Chogi hanmi kwangae Jeajomyung*, 25n8.

Princess Royal was built for the Glasgow and Liverpool Steam Packet Co., in 1861. Her general appearance was much more that of a blockade-runner than an Irish Channel steamer, and it is more than probable that she was built for blockade running purposes. The profits were so fantastically large that one or two successful trips more than repaid the speculators all their costs and expenses. The *Princess Royal* was sold to a Liverpool owner, who immediately began running the Federal blockade with her. . . .

Bought March 18, 1863 by the US Navy Department for $112,000, she was given a battery of two 30-pound Parrott rifles, one 11-inch Dahlgren gun and four 24-pound howitzers, being commissioned USS *Princess Royal* shortly afterwards. . . .

In the summer of 1865 USS *Princess Royal* was brought to Philadelphia and decommissioned, being sold at auction on August 17, 1885 to Samuel C. Cook for $54,175. . . . and in 1868 when Cook sold the *Princess Royal* to William F. Weld Co. of Boston, who were building up their Merchants of Boston SS Co. She was reconditioned and altered to fit her for this work, being also renamed the *General Sherman*. She was put into the New Orleans service with four other purchased steamers.

On January 4, 1874, the *General Sherman* left New York on her usual run with four passengers and a crew of forty-two men. Her cargo consisted of general merchandise consigned to New Orleans. The weather began to worsen and on January 7, 1874 at 2:00 AM the *General Sherman* sprung a bad leak, so that her pumps could not take care of the water pouring into her . . . when she sank.[40]

The *General Sherman* and the *Princess Royal* have several key differences.

First, the *Princess Royal* was built in 1861 and operated until it sank at 4:00 p.m. on January 8, 1874.

Second, the *Princess Royal* was renamed the *General Sherman* in 1868 when Samuel C. Cook sold it to William F. Weld of Boston. Therefore, if this was the ship that Thomas took to Korea in 1866, its name should have been the *Princess Royal*.

Third, records of their dimensions show that the *Princess Royal* and the *General Sherman*[41] that went to Korea are not the same vessel. The fol-

---

40. Heyl, "Early American Steamers," 351–52.
41. The dimension of the schooner is the length 178'9", width 49'7," and height 29'8".

lowing table compares the *Princess Royal* and the *General Sherman* that visited Korea.

Table 2. Comparison table between the *General Sherman* and the *Princess Royal*
(Units: feet and ton)

	Length	Width	Height	Tonnage
The *Princess Royal*	198'9"	27'3"	16'	619
The *General Sherman*	178'9"	49'7"	29'8"	60–80

Notably, the two ships showed a significant difference in weight. US government records list two different tonnages for the *General Sherman* that came to Korea. When the *General Sherman* incident occurred, US diplomat Anson Burlingame (1820–1870) requested US Rear Admiral Henry H. Bell (1808–1868) to investigate the matter. Rear Admiral Bell dispatched Shufeldt, the captain of the *Wachusett*, to Korea to investigate the facts regarding the *General Sherman*.[42] According to Shufeldt's report, the *General Sherman* was an 80-ton class merchant ship. The vessel was equipped with two 12-pound cannons, and the crew was armed.[43] In April 1868, Febiger, the captain of the *Shenandoah*, came to Korea again to check for survivors of the *General Sherman* incident. After completing his investigation, which included sending an official letter to the Korean government, Febiger mentioned in his report that the *General Sherman* was approximately 80 tons.[44]

In summary, the *General Sherman*'s tonnage was between 60 and 80 tons, whereas the *Princess Royal*'s tonnage was 619 tons. Therefore, the *Princess Royal* and the *General Sherman* are different ships.

William Tecumsch Sherman (1820–1891) was a Union general during the American Civil War (1861–1865) and is regarded as a pioneer of modern warfare. After the Civil War, many American naval vessels were named

---

It has two masts, one is height 149'1" and the other 128'2". Both big-sails are white in color. They are linked to two white small-sails by two ropes. The blue colored lifesaving boat has the length 14'7" and width 10'. Pak, *Jang-kea*, Aug. 22, 1866.

42. Maclay, *History of the United States Navy*, 4.

43. "*Shufeldt's Letter Book*, (No. 41), R. W. Shufeldt to rear Admiral H. H. Bell, USS *Wachusett*, Chefoo, Jan. 19, 1867," cited in Kim, *Kundae Hanmi Kwangea-sa*, 216.

44. "Febiger Letters, US Steamer *Shenandoah*, Chefoo, China, May 19, 1868. John C. Febiger to rear Admiral Stephen C. Rowan, Commanding US Asiatic Station, US Flag Ship *Piscataqua*," cited in Kim, *Kundae Hanmi Kwangea-sa*, 250.

General Sherman in his honor.⁴⁵ Some existing ships were also renamed the *General Sherman*, with the *Princess Royal* being one of them.

In a publication by Mutsu Munemitsu (1844–1897), who served as Japan's Minister of Foreign Affairs, there is a record stating that a *General Sherman* was the ship of Henry Andres Burgevine (1836–1865), a commander of the "Ever Victorious Army of China." Burgevine went to China aboard the *General Sherman* to carry out a mission to support the Taiping Rebellion.⁴⁶

In 1860, an attempt by the Taiping forces to reestablish their military prowess by taking Shanghai was halted by the Ever Victorious Army, which fought for the Qing Dynasty. The commander of this army was the American adventurer Frederick Townsend Ward (1831–1862).⁴⁷ However, Commander Ward died in September 1862, and his second-in-command, Burgevine, became the commander, going under the command of Lee Hongzhang (1823–1901) of the Qing government. Burgevine disagreed with Lee Hongzhang on the matter of salaries for the Ever Victorious Army and began a clandestine deal with the Taiping Rebellion Army.

In 1864, Burgevine was arrested by the Chinese army, together with Garingra, a British national. The consuls of Britain and America in Shanghai expelled Burgevine from China. On his way to the United States, he stopped in Yokohama, Japan. While there, he decided to return to China to help the Taiping Army. He recruited foreign mercenaries in Formosa (Taiwan) and acquired the American ship the *General Sherman*, which he subsequently armed.

Later, Burgevine was arrested again by the Chinese government's army when he tried to make an alliance with the Taiping Army.⁴⁸ It is known that Burgevine drowned with ten Qing policemen in the Xiamen Sea on his way

---

45. There is another record of a *General Sherman* in Silverstone, *Warships of the Civil War Navies*. The *General Sherman* was built in 1864 and it had the length 51.21m, width 8m, height 1.46m, and weight 187 tons. There is a note under the photograph of the *General Sherman* as follows: "The *General Sherman*, one of the four side-wheels steamers built by the Army and converted to tin-clad" (US Naval Historical Centre). Therefore, this *General Sherman* is not the same as the *General Sherman* that went to Korea. Silverstone, *Warships of the Civil War Navies*, 167.

46. Munemitsu, *Geonjeong-rok*, 195.

47. *New Encyclopaedia Britannica*, 11:509.

48. Munemitsu, *Geonjeong-rok*, 195.

to Shanghai, although some historians believed that he was murdered on Li Hongzhang's orders.[49]

The *General Sherman* was moved to Tientsin by the Chinese government and sold to an American named Preston. It is clear that the *General Sherman* was not armed specifically for a trip to Korea; it had already been armed by Burgevine. Preston then acquired this heavily armed vessel and repurposed it as a merchant ship.

2) How Many People Were On Board the *General Sherman*?

The number of people on board the *General Sherman* has long been a subject of debate. The figures presented in studies on the *General Sherman* and Thomas vary, including nineteen,[50] five to twenty,[51] twenty,[52] twenty-two,[53] twenty-three,[54] twenty-four,[55] an twenty-seven.[56] The earliest record lists twenty people, as documented in *Jang-kea*. The next record is a report from Sanford, the US Consul in Shanghai, to Burlingame, the US envoy in Peking. Sanford estimated the number of *General Sherman* crew members to be between fifteen and twenty. The figure of twenty-four first appeared in a document sent from Williams, the acting US diplomat in Peking, to the Chinese foreign office (Zongli Yamen). When this document was delivered to the Korean government via the foreign office, the Korean government records were also changed to twenty-four.[57]

The Korean government's first record is *Jang-kea* dated August 22, 1866, which reports on a conversation between Thomas and Kim Nak-soo and Jo Won-gook, who visited the *General Sherman*.

---

49. *Oxford Dictionary of National Biography*, 22:865.

50. Gale, "Fate of the *General Sherman*," 252.

51. Mr. Sandford to Mr. Burlingame, Oct. 30, 1866, Chefoo.

52. *Ilseongnok Diary* (daily observations of the Korean king between 1752 to 1910), Aug. 27, 1866.

53. McCune, *Korean-American Relations*, 46.

54. Oh, *Thomas Moksa-jeon*, 39

55. Rhodes, *History of the Korea Mission*, 74; Mr. Williamson to Foreign Office, Legation of the United States, Oct. 23, 1866; Griffis, *Corea, the Hermit Nation*, 394.

56. *Shufeldt Letter Book*, (No. 43), Memoranda, USS *Wachusett*, Wachusett Bay, Near Mouth of Tai-tong River, Corea, Jan. 25, 1867; Anson Burlingame to Rev. Robert Thomas, Apr. 23, 1867, in *Cambrian* [Welsh newspaper], July 26, 1867.

57. *Gojong Taehwangje Sillok*, Nov. 5, 1866.

> Kim Nak-soo, Jo Won-gook: How many of you are on the ship other than you four? Are there any other foreigners other than westerners?
>
> Thomas: There are 20 of us, 13 Chinese, 2 blacks and 5 westerners.[58]

Thomas stated that all 20 people on board the *General Sherman* had departed from China. This report is a government record dated August 27, included in *Ilseongnok*. At the time, it was delivered from Pyongyang to the royal palace in the capital by a mounted messenger. Consequently, there was an inevitable difference between the date of the report from Pyongyang and the date of the record in the capital. Furthermore, the *Jang-kea* contains detailed records of the number of casualties and the manner in which they died when the *General Sherman* was burned:

> Our soldiers searched for the enemies who had escaped the burning ship and shot them. When we counted them afterwards, we shot 13 of them to death and 4 of them were burned to death, including 1, who had been shot to death before, total number of the enemy was 20.[59]

Thomas noted that there were twenty people on board the *General Sherman*, including themselves, and records indicate that twenty of the crew died after the ship was burned. Therefore, it can be concluded that the *General Sherman* had a crew of twenty.

Among the crew of the *General Sherman* that left Tientsin were W. B. Preston (the owner of the schooner), Page (the master of the vessel), and Wilson (the mate).[60] It seems that the mate Wilson was a naturalized American from Denmark. On July 29, thirteen of them left Tientsin. There were three Americans, eight Southern-Chinese men, and two Malaysian black men.[61]

At Chefoo, two British—Hogarth, the cargo-responsible representative of Messrs. Meadows & Co., and Thomas—boarded the ship. Thomas also brought one Chinese from Peking,[62] and there was one Cantonese

---

58. Pak, *Jang-kea*, Aug. 22, 1866.
59. Pak, *Jang-kea*, Sept. 2, 1866.
60. Mr. Sandford to Mr. Buringame, Oct. 30, 1866, Chefoo.
61. According to *Jang-kea* ("Record of the Pyengan Army Camp"), Thomas said that there were two black men, one from Philippines and one from Thailand. However, a letter from Messrs. Meadows & Co. to the British consul says that there were South Chinese men and Malaysians. Therefore, the two Blacks are the Malaysians.
62. According to the letter of Edkins and Pauline Morache, there was one Peking

shroff[63] from Messrs. Meadows & Co. In addition, two pilots from Shantung boarded. Therefore, a total of seven people boarded the ship at Chefoo. By nationality, there were two British, three American (including one naturalized Danish), two Malaysian, and thirteen Chinese (one Cantonese, two from Shantung, and ten from Southern China).

3) Did Thomas Go to Pyongyang to Meet Pak Kyu-su?

In the history of Korean Christianity, it is commonly accepted that Pak Kyu-su (1807–1877) met Thomas during his journey to Peking as part of the Dongjisa mission.[64] The book *Thomas Moksa-jon* (Reverend Thomas's Biography), written by Oh Moon-hwan in 1928, records that when Pak Kyu-su visited Peking with the Dongjisa delegation, he received a Bible as a gift from Thomas and promised to help him when he visited Pyongyang:

> Thomas who was preaching the Gospel in Korea for only two and a half months resided in Peking. Occasionally, a thought entered his mind. It was that he would plan another trip to Korea to preach the Gospel again. In the very nick of time, he heard that Pak Kyu-su who was a member of the annual Korean Embassy stayed in Peking. He visited in haste him and presented him a bible. Thomas said, "Blessings will come home to you, if you accept and live in accordance with what this book says." After a lengthy conversation, Thomas asked, "I wish you to help me in various ways on that occasion I go to Korea again." Pak Kyu-su gave his word to Thomas. After coming back to Korea, he gave the bible to Kim Ok-gyun, and Kim Ok-gyun gave it to Kim Hong-jip. His plan for a second mission trip to Korea is well known through his letter. In NBSS report of 1866, "Revd Thomas implemented the mission of this society. He sailed along the coast adventurously

person assisting Thomas. However, the record of Messrs. Meadows & Co. says there were two of them. "Mr. Thomas, we understood, took two Pekingese with him." It is believed that there was confusion in Messrs. Meadows & Co. Their information on the number of the *General Sherman* crew was sixteen to twenty. It seems that the record of Edkins and Pauline Morache is consistent. The Korean government record says that the last person who stayed with Thomas was a Peking person, Jo Neung-bong.

63. These shroffs were experts in handling money. They could detect counterfeits by the touch, and, with incredible celerity, reckon amounts to thousandths of a cent on the abacus. One or more of them were found in nearly every one of the banks and hongs in Eurasian ports (Griffis, *Corea, the Hermit Nation*, 391).

64. Kim, *Chogi Hanmi Gwangyeui Jaejomyeong*, 30

mixing with Korean merchants, and one of them even said that if he came back the next year he would guide him to the capital city. Thomas handed out many copies of the Bible while going about the west coast, and also procured many books in Korean to collect the dialects until he could speak the language of the capital city to some degree." It is certain that his plan became clear. The plan became finalized through the meeting with Pak Kyu-su. The fact of the meeting between Thomas and Pak Kyu-su in Peking is testified by Lee Hyuk-nam (Joyang-ri, Chori-myeon, Gangseo-gun, Pyeongnam; around 100 years old if he were still alive), who had a close relationship with high-ranking officials of the government then, and by other four or five persons. According to Kim Jeong-gyu (address: Songo-ri, Chori-myeon, Gangseo-gun), who had boarded the boat in person and communicated with Thomas while Thomas stopped at Bosan. Thomas referred to Pak Kyu-su as his relative.[65]

In the book *PyengyangJinsil* (The Truth of Pyeongyang), it is stated multiple times that Thomas met Pak Kyu-su in Peking in April.[66] However, the author of *PyengyangJinsil* remains unidentified.[67] Kim Yang-sun also records that Thomas met Pak Kyu-su in Peking.[68]

Pak Kyu-su was the grandson of Pak Ji-weon (1737–1805), a leading scholar of the Korean Bukhak-sect.[69] Pak Ji-weon gained fame by publishing the *Yelha-ilki* (Journal of Rehe) in 1780 after visiting Rehe province as part of the annual Korean Embassy, where Emperor Qianlong (1735–1796) resided during his summer retreat. Pak Ji-weon also authored numerous works, establishing himself as a founder of Silhak (practical science).

Pak Kyu-su was a follower of Silhak and a pioneer of enlightenment thought.[70] At forty-two, he passed the state examination, entering politics.

---

65. Oh, *Thomas Moksa-jeon*, 29–30.

66. Kim, *Chogi hanmi kwangae Jeajomyung*, 32.

67. Kim, *Chogi hanmi kwangae Jeajomyung*, 31.

68. Kim, *Hanguk Gyohisa Yeongu*, 44.

69. Since Korean intellectuals internalized Sinocentrism by accepting Ming culture and institutions enthusiastically, this brought prejudice against another culture and people. Even 130 years after the fall of Ming, they still followed toadyism toward Ming, enslaved by closed thinking, unable to grasp the international situation newly changing around Ching. At this time, Bukak-sect is a political faction in the Korea era that insisted on advancing Korea by accepting China's culture and institutions positively. Woo, Joseon "Junghwajueui-e daehan Hakseolsajeok Geomto," 237–44.

70. Kim, *Chogi hanmi kwangae Jeajomyung*, 12.

The Second Visit to Korea

From February 1866 to April 1869, he served as the governor of Pyongan Province. During his tenure, the *General Sherman* incident occurred, and Pak Kyu-su played a leading role in this event. Following the incident, he was responsible for managing relations with the United States.

Pak Kyu-su did not go to Peking with the Dongjisa delegation in 1866. He visited Peking on two separate occasions. His first visit was in 1861, when he was appointed as the deputy envoy of a mission sent by the government to comfort the Xianfeng Emperor, who had fled to Rehe due to the Second Opium War.[71] He departed for China on January 18, 1861, and returned to Korea on June 19 of the same year.[72] His second visit was in 1872, when Pak Kyu-su went to Peking as the ambassador of the annual Korean Embassy.[73]

Pak Kyu-su did not go to Peking in either 1865 or 1866. The claim that Thomas went to Pyongyang to meet Pak Kyu-su is a distorted one.

There is a possibility that the person named Pak, whom Thomas met in Peking and who claimed to have read the book Thomas had distributed on the West Coast, was mistaken for Pak Kyu-su. However, in a letter written by Thomas himself, this person is recorded as "a merchant named Pakka" who accompanied the Dongjisa delegation. Pak Kyu-su was a high-ranking official and could not have been confused with someone of the "merchant" class. Pak Kyu-su was not part of the Dongjisa.

Trade with China began to significantly impact the Korean economy starting in the mid-seventeenth century. During this period, envoys traveling to the Qing Dynasty were called Yeonhaengsa. Regular diplomatic missions included the Dongjihaeng and Yeokhaeng, and the envoys who participated in the Dongjihaeng were called Dongjisa. The Dongjisa would arrive in Peking for the Lunar New Year, having departed from Seoul in the 10th month of the lunar calendar and returning around the 4th month of the following year. The official Dongjisa mission dispatched by the government consisted of a Chief Envoy, a Deputy Envoy, and a Document Officer, with a formal staff of about thirty-five people. However, when officials' servants, horsemen, porters, and merchants looking to trade were included, the total number reached two hundred to three hundred people. For the merchants seeking trade, the Dongjihaeng was a crucial opportunity to

---

71. *Cheoljong Sillok* [Annals of King Cheoljong], Dec. 9, 1861; *Ilseongnok*, Dec. 9, 1861.

72. *Journal of Korean Government Secret Service*, Feb. 17, 1861 and July 26, 1861.

73. Kim, *Hwanjae Pak Kyu-Su*, 12.

travel to China in large numbers. On the Dongjisa's journey from Seoul to Peking, horsemen and merchants were recruited in Pyongyang.[74] Therefore, Pakka, who had the surname Pak, was a merchant who came with the Dongjisa delegation selected in Pyongyang.

On April 19, 1866, Alexander Williamson met a company of the annual Korean Embassy returning to Korea at Tien-chwang-tai in the Liaotung area. One member of the Korean Embassy, who spoke Mandarin Chinese fluently, said that he had met many missionaries in Peking as well as visited the LMS.[75] This report agrees with what Thomas's letter says.

In Peking, Thomas was successfully carrying out his mission as a pioneering missionary. In July 1866, he was invited by the French Embassy to participate as an interpreter in the French fleet's visit to Korea.

4) Was Thomas Responsible for the *General Sherman* incident?

When Febiger arrived in Korea to investigate the *General Sherman* incident, the Korean government informed him that "Thomas had illegally entered our country aboard a foreign vessel."[76] This suggested that Thomas played a major role on the *General Sherman*. In his August 16 report, Jeong Dae-sik noted, "Thomas was in charge of everything on board,"[77] and two days later, Yu Cho-hwan described him as "the leader of the foreigners."[78] Han Gyoo-moo viewed Thomas not as just an interpreter but as a key figure who decided the ship's course. As a result, Han Gyoo-moo held Thomas accountable for what happened to the *General Sherman* on the Daedong River.[79]

Thomas spoke a bit of Korean and was fluent in Chinese, which meant he was central to virtually all interactions with Koreans. Consequently, Koreans tended to exaggerate his influence and assumed he must have been the captain of the *General Sherman*.

---

74. Guksapyeonchan Wiwonhoe, *Geosang, Jeonguk Sanggwon-eul Jangakhada*, 207.

75. Williamson, *Journeys in North China*, 131.

76. "Febiger Letters, 'B.' Sam Hoa, District Magistrate, Le to the Honorable American. Mou Chin, Third Month, Twenty-fifth," cited in Kim, *Chogi hanmi kwangae Jeajomyung*, 241.

77. *Gojong Taehwangje Sillok*, Aug. 24, 1866.

78. Pak, *Jang-ke*, Aug. 8 1866.

79. Han, "*General Sherman* Sagunkwa Thomas Sunkyomoonje," 15.

The Second Visit to Korea

A comparable case exists in which the Korean government mistook an interpreter for the actual commander. On October 11, 1866, a French squadron departed Chefoo and occupied Ganghwa Island with seven warships and approximately one thousand troops. Capitaine de vaisseau Olivier of the French Navy assembled a contingent of 160 men for a special operation. Catholic priest Ridel—known in Korea as Lee Bong-myung—guided Olivier's force to Jeongjok Mountain Fortress. However, they were ambushed by Yang Heon-su's unit, resulting in six French fatalities and thirty-two wounded. The blow shattered French morale and prompted a withdrawal. Government records state that "Lee was the commander of the French troops."[80] Although Admiral Rose oversaw the naval squadron and Capitaine de vaisseau Olivier led the assault upon Jeongjok Mountain, Korean officials recorded Ridel as the commanding figure. Pak Kyu-su likewise noted that "the bearded man who spoke Korean was the captain of the French force,"[81] attributing leadership to someone he assumed held command due to his language skills.

That said, it is necessary to consider the later testimony of Wu Wen Tai—in a letter to Consul Mongan of Messrs. Meadows & Co.—who recounted having met Thomas at the mouth of the Daedong River:

> He (Wu Wen Tai) is 43 years of age, and has traded for many years with Corea. "Mr. Thomas constantly wanted to land and ramble about, but the pilot advised him against doing so." Thomas wished to keep the pilot and let his junk return to Shantung, but his junkmen would not hear of it, saying they could not face his family without him. On the pilot reaching the mouth of the Ping Yang River he had some conversation with the Coreans there, and they told him that their Sovereign would by no means trade with foreigners. My teacher (Thomas) acted as Interpreter during the above conversation, which lasted a good time.[82]

From the records above, we can draw the following conclusions.

First, Thomas's activities were restricted during the initial visit to Korea. He was even prevented from disembarking to take a walk.

Second, Thomas became aware of the dangerous situation in Korea and believed the visit to Pyongyang was too risky. He proposed they return to the Shandong Peninsula, but the crew refused.

---

80. Kim, *Chogi hanmi kwangae Jeajomyung*, 105.
81. Kim, *Chogi hanmi kwangae Jeajomyung*, 105.
82. Extract from Mr. Mackey's letter to Messrs. Meadows & Co., Oct. 8, 1866, Chefoo.

The First Protestant Martyr in Korea from Wales

Third, Thomas's role on the *General Sherman* was merely that of an interpreter. The Koreans Wu Wen Tai saw visiting the *General Sherman* at the mouth of the Daedong River were Lee Gil-ho and Shin Bong-jin. Lee Gil-ho and Shin Bong-jin reported that Lee Pal-haeng made the decisions, and Thomas interpreted for him. In other words, Thomas was Lee Pal-haeng's interpreter.[83] Another record states that Lee Pal-haeng was the owner of the *General Sherman*.[84] However, the ship's actual owner was Preston, and Thomas was his interpreter. Still other Korean records indicate that Thomas wanted to leave Korea. Between three and five o'clock in the afternoon on August 23, Lee Hyun-ik and Shin Tae-jeong boarded the *General Sherman* and engaged in the following conversation:

> About 20 li (7.8 km) upstream from Pyongyang—just past Sin-jang Port near Duru Island—Commander Lee Hyun-ik and Chief Magistrate of Pyongyang Shin Tae-jeong boarded the ship and declared, "You've refused to turn back and continue upriver, so we must have a formal discussion with you." The ship's crew replied, "We will turn the ship around after we have traded for local products." The officials then stated, "Trade with foreign countries is forbidden by our country's laws, so you must first gain permission from the Chinese emperor before you can be received here. While it is fitting for us to supply your ship with anything you may lack or need, trade is not something that can be conducted as you please." It seemed the Westerners, Thomas and Cho Nung-bong, were somewhat inclined to listen and comply. However, the ship owner (Preston) and the cargo owner (Hogarth) were both stubbornly insistent on trading.[85]

This report indicates that Thomas lacked the authority to make final decisions, which suggests he was not the captain of the *General Sherman*. Furthermore, an intriguing record from Admiral Shufeldt notes that the British Hogarth was known for his "reckless character." It's possible that Hogarth was responsible for the unrest caused by the *General Sherman* in Pyongyang.[86]

---

83. *Gojong Taehwangje Sillok*, Aug. 24, 1866.

84. Pak, *Jang-kea*, Aug. 22, 1866. Lee Pal-haeng said he was the owner of the ship and he was from Denmark. In addition, there were three Americans and two British. Among them, Wilson was a naturalized American from Denmark.

85. Pak, *Jang-kea*, Aug. 24, 1866.

86. Kim, *Kundae Hanmi Kwangea-sa*, 220.

5) On What Date Was Thomas Martyred?

Generally, Thomas's date of martyrdom is recorded as either September 2 or September 5, 1866, since the exact date remains unclear. This uncertainty stems from the limitations in the process of gathering and analyzing sources. The two principal primary records that document his martyrdom are the *Gojong Taehwangje Sillok* and the *Ilseongnok*; both assign the date as September 5, 1866 (the 27th day of the 7th lunar month in Gojong's third year). However, these entries are based on the *Jang-kea* submitted by Pak Kyu-su, the governor of Pyongyang. In the September 5 entries of both the *Gojong Taehwangje Sillok* and the *Ilseongnok*, the following is recorded: "The governor of Pyongyang reports that the people of Pyongyang burned the Western ship and killed the British Choi Nan-heon (Thomas)."

At that time, delivering *Jang-kea* report from Pyongyang to Hanyang via the state relay system—papalma—typically took about three to four days. Considering that Governor Pak Kyu-su submitted these reports every two to three days after the *General Sherman* entered Pyongyang, it appears he relied on the relay horses to communicate urgently with the central government during the crisis.

Assuming Governor Pak's *Jang-kea*—which records the *General Sherman*'s final destruction on the Daedong River and Thomas's death—is the most trustworthy primary account, it is reasonable to infer that Thomas was martyred on September 2, 1866. Roughly three days later, the news would have reached the court via papalma, leading to its entry in the *Gojong Taehwangje Sillok* under September 5. To date, most historical research has overlooked this delay between when *Jang-kea* was penned and when it reached the capital.

5. THE KIDNAPPING OF LEE HYUN-IK AND THE FATE OF THE *GENERAL SHERMAN*

Between 5:00 p.m. and 7:00 p.m. on August 27, six foreigners left the *General Sherman* and climbed into a small boat to head upstream. The military officer Lee Hyun-ik, accompanied by Yoo Soon-won and Park Chi-yeong, followed them in a separate boat.[87] Lee stayed close, intent on preventing any confrontations between Koreans and foreigners.[88] Suddenly, the Sher-

---

87. Pak, *Jang-kea*, Aug. 28, 1866.
88. *Shufeldt's Letter Book*, "C," The Intendant of Circuit in the Hwang Hae District

man's crew seized Lee and the two Korean aides and forcibly took them aboard the main ship. The Chief Magistrate of Pyongyang insisted their release—but the crew refused.

The next morning, August 28, the *General Sherman* moved upstream and began firing its guns and cannons. Five crew members left the *General Sherman* and headed in the direction of Otan in a small boat. At that time, residents of Pyongyang gathered along the riverbank and signaled for Lee Hyun-ik to be returned. The crew of the *General Sherman* responded that they would enter the city and discuss the matter. Furious, the Koreans began throwing stones, and the soldiers in the city fired arrows and guns. The foreigners abandoned their small boat and returned to the *General Sherman*. The *General Sherman* was anchored downstream of Yanggakdo, a small island on the Daedong River. At approximately 4:00 p.m., a retired official, Park Chun-gwon, successfully rescued Lee. Tragically, Yoo Soon-won and Park Chi-yeong—who had jumped into the river—are presumed lost.[89]

In 1867, Admiral Shufeldt investigated the *General Sherman* incident and concluded that the ship had flouted official orders from Korean authorities and sailed all the way to Pyongyang. He argued that the entire incident began with the crew's provocatively precursory kidnapping of Lee Hyun-ik, which sparked a Korean attack that resulted in the execution of the foreigners.[90]

According to *Paegangrok* (Record of the Pae River), another Korean approached the *Sherman* first: Ahn Sang-hop, who carried a document outlining a plan for dealing with the ship. Shufeldt notes that the crew acquired this document—and later claimed they kidnapped Lee in response, fearing the Koreans intended to massacre them.[91]

Meanwhile, *Jang-kea* reports state that through August 30, Korean officials continued attempting to persuade the *Sherman* to depart peacefully—without violence:

> It's already several days but the schooner does not go away. Mangyeong Gazebo is less than 20 li from Pyengyang castle. We tried to persuade them to leave but they don't listen. We don't

---

to Commander Shufeldt, fifth year of the emperor Tung Chi, twelfth month, diplomatic materials in Kim, *Kundae Hanmi Kwangea-sa*, 225.

89. Pak, *Jang-kea*, Aug. 28, 1866.
90. Shufeldt, "Corea's Troubles."
91. Kim, *Hanguk Kyohoe-sa Yŭngu*, 45.

The Second Visit to Korea

know their thought or intention. We keep stricter guard and observation.[92]

They now know that Korea does not want to trade and they should go away. But they keep coming up the river. We don't know their intention.[93]

On September 1, a formal plan was adopted to attack the *General Sherman*.[94] All government officials conducting the investigation operated under the authority of Governor Pak Kyu-su. Once Lee Hyun-ik was kidnapped, tensions snapped and open hostility followed. When the *General Sherman* first approached Pyongyang, it was the rainy season, and heavy rains made an investigation impossible.[95] As time passed, the rainy season ended, and the water level of the Daedong River dropped. On August 28, the *General Sherman* moved slightly downstream from Hansa Gazebo. The ship was anchored downstream of Yanggakdo and no longer moved.

A critical concern for the crew was dwindling food supplies. By August 31, desperate for provisions, they attacked a local merchant vessel on the river. In the skirmish, seven Koreans were killed and five wounded. During that encounter, Kim Bong-jo shot and killed one of the *Sherman*'s sailors—the very first recorded death among the crew.

Pak Kyu-su reported that he had attempted to take the *General Sherman* crew as prisoners, but the ship's superior firepower made it difficult.[96] The fighting continued on that day, with the *General Sherman* positioned about 328 yards downstream from Yanggakdo. Korean forces fired guns and arrows from the riverbank, while the ship responded with cannon fire. Though the *General Sherman*'s crew was small in number, the vessel's height—about thirty feet above the water—made it resemble attacking a fortress.

Late that night, Pak announced, "We have just finalized our plan to drive them off."[97] In the early morning hours of September 2, the *General Sherman* drifted slightly upriver to a point about 218 yards downstream from Yanggakdo and remained anchored.

---

92. Pak, *Jang-kea*, Aug. 24, 1866.
93. Pak, *Jang-kea*, Aug. 27, 1866.
94. Pak, *Jang-kea*, Sept. 1, 1866.
95. Pak, *Jang-kea*, Aug. 20, 1866.
96. Pak, *Jang-kea*, Aug. 31, 1866.
97. Pak, *Jang-kea*, Sept. 1, 1866.

Around noon, the ship crew killed another Korean—prompting Korean soldiers and civilians to launch a coordinated assault. They prepared rafts loaded with wood, straw, and—crucially—gunpowder, setting them adrift toward the *General Sherman*. Once the rafts struck the hull, the gunpowder ignited. Under the signal of Korean combatants, these burning rafts floated in from both sides of the river, colliding with the ship and triggering explosions. Finally, the *General Sherman* was engulfed in flames.[98]

6. THE END OF THOMAS

After Korea and the United States signed the Treaty of Amity and Commerce, American navy lieutenant J. B. Bernadon traveled from Pyongyang to Hanyang in 1884.

> The angry government officials and people began to attack the General Sherman. The General Sherman surrendered with a white flag but it had already caught fire. Crew who jumped into the water mostly drowned to death. Some were caught alive including Thomas. As Thomas spoke some Korean, he explained that he had surrendered with a white flag. He pleaded with the Koreans to hand them over to the Chinese; however, that was in vain.[99]

In 1884, there were officially no missionaries in Korea. What lends this testimony its strength is that it was recorded without knowledge that Thomas had ever been a missionary. James S. Gale subsequently wrote the following:

> The wretched foreigners were now hacked to pieces by the furious mob. One or two who reached shore carried a white flag, which they waved while they bowed repeatedly. But no quarter was given, they were pinioned and cut to pieces, then the remains were still further mutilated, certain parts were cut off to be used as medicine, the rest were gathered up and burned in a heap.[100]

According to Lieutenant J. B. Bernadon, it was Thomas who raised the white flag and surrendered. Oh Moon-hwan's account of Thomas's death appears below:

---

98. Kim, *Kundae Hanmi Kwangea-sa*, 225.
99. Griffis, *Corea, the Hermit Nation*, 392.
100. Gale, "Fate of the *General Sherman*," 254.

The Second Visit to Korea

> While Thomas was throwing Bibles from the ship, the General Sherman caught fire with smoke. He knew that he would be killed if he left the ship; however, he thought that he would tell the gospel to the soldier who would kill him. He took one Bible and got out of the ship. One soldier jumped on him. Thomas offered the Bible to the soldier and he kneeled on the beach for prayer. After the prayer, he stood up and offered the Bible again to the soldier. The soldier did not understand what Thomas meant. He took away Thomas' life by the sword.[101]

There's a common thread in the contemporary accounts by James Gale, Lieutenant Bernadon, and Oh Moon-hwan: they each state that Thomas came off the ship and was killed. And if you look closely at *Jang-kea* concerning Thomas's final fate, it likewise reports that both Thomas and Cho Nung-bong disembarked and were put to death:

> Around noon, their ship opened fire with cannons and guns, killing one of our people. Instantly, both civilians and soldiers across the city let out a unified battle-cry and launched an assault. They then dispatched multiple fireships simultaneously—setting the ship aflame with incendiaries—and burned it completely. Among the crew, Thomas and Cho Nung-bong ran to the bow, pleading for their lives. They were taken and brought to a hill by the river, but the enraged crowd and soldiers, furious at the sight of them, killed them on the spot. They killed Thomas and Cho Nung-bong.[102]

Missionary Thomas carried lots of the Bible with him. While he was in China, he taught from Scripture every day. It's quite possible he still had a Bible with him at the very end—and may even have tried to hand one over before he died. This is the testimony of Han Seok-jin, sent to Oh Moon-hwan on January 16, 1928:

> I traveled to Pyongyang for the first time in October 1892. It was the twenty-sixth anniversary of Thomas's death. If I had made an effort to search out any trace of Missionary Thomas back then, I might have learned more—but I was only working as a colporteur, and I simply listened to what local people told me during my ministry. Those who witnessed the incident said that a foreigner who had been standing on deck shouted "Jesus!" and that, while the foreign ship was ablaze, this man hurled a large number of books

---

101. Oh, "Two Visits," 57–58.
102. Pak, *Jang-kea*, Sept. 2, 1866.

onto the shore. Later, they told me that the books I was selling matched exactly the ones that that foreigner had thrown.[103]

On September 10, 1866, Pak Kyu-su concluded his formal report on the *General Sherman* incident with the following statement:

> I already reported that most of the things on the ship were burnt. The schooner was burnt; therefore, the weapons and steel bar on the ship became unusable. We found things as much as possible in the water or even burnt. Cannon, iron anchors and iron chains are relatively in good shape; however, other steel or iron things were melted and sent to the armory. The following had been sent to the armory. Two cannon, two small cannon, three cannon balls, two iron anchors, 793 feet of small and big iron chains, 780 kg iron, 1410 kg of iron rods, 1287 kg of scrap iron.[104]

The iron chains taken from the *General Sherman* were hung between the pillars of the East Gate of Pyongyang Fortress as a commemorative trophy of victory.[105] Thomas died in Pyongyang, just eighteen days after departing from the mouth of the Daedong River.

> Messrs. Meadows & Co. to Mr. Burlingame[106]
> Tientsin, October 27, 1866
>
> Sir:
>
> We, the undersigned British firm, beg leave to bring to your Excellency's notice the following circumstances, in order to obtain your Excellency's assistance in getting redress.
> During the latter half of July last, the American Schooner *General Sherman* arrived at this port, and was consigned to, our care by Mr. Preston, the owner, who had come passenger on the vessel for the sake of his health. After we had taken delivery of inward cargo, Mr. Preston and we came to an arrangement that we should load her with a cargo of foreign merchandise, and dispatch her to Korea with a super-cargo to sell the goods there. We accordingly loaded her with foreign merchandise, and on 29th of July last she left Tientsin. Mr. Hogarth, one of our clerks, who

---

103. Oh, "Two Visits," 121.

104. Pak, *Jang-kea*, Sept. 10 1866. Goh Moo-song recorded: "162 lengths of iron chain, 130 lbs iron, 2,250 lbs iron rods, 2,145 lbs of scrap iron." But Goh's record is wrong because he just changed the Korean units to English units without conversion of values.

105. Gale, "Fate of the General Sherman," 254.

106. Oh, "Two Visits," 174–176. Anson Burlingame was the United States Minister Plenipotentiary.

went as super-cargo, left previously in the steamer *Shaftesbury* for Chefoo, in order to have a pilot and shroff ready on the "*General Sherman*" arriving there, and thus save delay. On the schooner reaching Chefoo, Mr. Hogarth, accompanied by a Chinese pilot and a Cantonese shroff belonging to our firm, went on board; also Mr. Thomas, who having expressed a wish to visit Korea again, in order to extend his knowledge of Korean language, went as passenger. From the day the vessel left Chefoo till now, we have received no written advices from Mr. Hogarth or Mr. Preston, or in fact, from any one on board when she let Chefoo.

On the 8th of October current, we received letters from the partners of our firm in Chefoo, with the news that the King of Corea had caused the *General Sherman* to be burnt with all on board, while proceeding up the Ping Yang river.

We immediately addressed Dr. Williams on the subject copy of our letter herewith enclosed.

On the 20th of October current, we received further advices from our partner in Chefoo, informing us that he had seen a junk captain who had piloted the schooner for four tides up the Ping Yang river, when he left her and returned to the mouth of the river to his junk, and finally to Chefoo. This man stated that the Koreans had told him their king was opposed to foreign intercourse with his country. We imagine that this man, who understands something of the Korean language, knows something more about the vessel than he is inclined to divulge, fearing, Chinese-like, to mix himself up in the matter with the authorities to question him later on the points.

As the act of visiting Korea for the purposes of trade was not an act which could, in the eyes of civilized western nations, justify the Korean government in destroying those who committed it, we, the undersigned, have takes the liberty of addressing you for the purpose of bringing the above matters to your Excellency's notice, with the request that you will be pleased to beg his Excellency Admiral Bell to make inquiries regarding the destruction of the vessel and her people, and take steps to cause the Korean Government to make redress as far as such in the nature of things is practicable.

We have the honor to be, sir, your Excellency's most obedient servants,

Meadows & Co.

Chapter 7

The Martyrdom of Thomas and His Missionary Legacy

DRIVEN BY A FIERY zeal for the gospel, Thomas made two missionary journeys to Korea and ultimately became the first Protestant martyr in Korean history. The fledgling church in Korea fully embraced his death as a sacred offering. In *History of the Korea Mission: Presbyterian Church U.S.A., 1884–1934*, his death is explicitly recorded as "the first Protestant martyr in Korea."[1] Likewise, the London-published *Congregational Year Book 1868* affirms that Thomas indeed was martyred.[2] As a martyr, Thomas left the Korean church a precious legacy of missionary heritage, which includes the following.

First, among Koreans who received the Bibles distributed by Thomas, some later became Christians. Samuel A. Moffett arrived in Korea in 1890 and made three visits to Pyongyang before, in 1893, he became the first Protestant missionary to take up long-term residence there. At the annual missionaries' conference in Seoul in October 1893, he reported as follows:

> I am doing God's work in Pyengyang and many important things happened. I learned that somebody already gave Bibles in Pyengyang and they had been read. People on the street and people in the city already had Bibles.[3]

---

1. Rhodes, *History of the Korea Mission*, 71–72
2. *Congregational Year Book 1868*, 298.
3. Lee, *Naraui Dokrip, Kyohoiui Dokrip*, 74.

The Martyrdom of Thomas and His Missionary Legacy

Among those who received a Bible from Thomas was an eleven-year-old boy named Choi Chi-ryang (1854–1930). Choi was baptized by Samuel Moffett in 1894 and became a Christian.[4] Later, Choi moved to Ochon-ri, where he established the Ochon-ri Church and founded the Kyungsin School with his own private funds. Hong Shin-gil (1848–?) also received a Bible from Thomas and later became an elder, founding the Hari Church. Park Chun-gwon (1839–1920), who had saved Lee Hyun-ik, was baptized by Moffett in 1899 and became the leader of Sin-am Church.[5] Additionally, a nephew of a relative who had received a Bible from Thomas later became a Christian and translated the Bible into Korean with the assistance of William D. Reynolds (1867–1951). These accounts are recorded in the autobiography of Sherwood Hall (1893–1991), the son of William James Hall (1860–1894), the first Methodist missionary in Pyongyang:

> Thomas gave a Bible to a Korean just before he died. He took the Bible to his home. His nephew later became a Christian and helped Reynolds in the translation of the Bible into Korean. Reynolds was a missionary from the PBFM (South).[6]

A New Testament brought to Korea by Thomas is currently housed at the Korean Christian Museum at Soongsil University in Korea. This particular Bible was the *Delegates Version*, which was printed in 1858 at the LMS press in Shanghai.[7] The LMS had established and operated this press since 1843. Between 1844 and 1860, the LMS press published 171 editions of books. Of these, 138 (80.7%) were Christian books, including Bibles, while 33 (19.3%) were related to Western medicine.[8] With the rapid spread of Christianity in Korea in the late nineteenth and early twentieth centuries, the belief that the Bibles Thomas shared were the seeds of the Korean church became a widely accepted idea.[9]

Second, the martyrdom of Thomas influenced John Ross (1841–1915), motivating him to undertake the translation of the first Korean Bible. John Ross was a missionary affiliated with the United Presbyterian Church of Scotland. On August 23, 1872, he traveled to Chefoo, China, to assist fellow

---

4. Lee, *Naraui Dokrip, Kyohoiui Dokrip*, 75.
5. Ryang, "First Protestant Missionary to Korea," 72.
6. Hall, *With a Stethoscope in Asia*, 75.
7. Sungsil Taehakkyo, *Korean Christian Museum*, 259.
8. Kim, *Jungkuk Kyohoe-sa*, 84.
9. Oak, *Making of Korean Christianity*, 72.

missionary Alexander Williamson, who was also from his denomination. Williamson informed Ross about Thomas's death in Korea, which sparked Ross's interest in the country and led him to learn more about its situation.[10] Williamson played a pivotal role in connecting Thomas and Ross, significantly impacting early Korean missions. In September 1867, a year after Thomas's death, Williamson embarked on a missionary journey to Manchuria. He visited the Goryeo Gate and distributed Bibles to Koreans he encountered.[11] Recognizing the importance of Manchuria for mission work, Williamson urged the mission board to send Ross there. Ross accepted the assignment and arrived in Yingkou, Manchuria, in October 1872. Ironically, Ross's wife passed away suddenly in 1873 while giving birth to their first child,[12] a situation reminiscent of Thomas's wife Caroline, who died during missionary work in Shanghai. Additionally, both Ross and Thomas shared Celtic heritage, with Ross being of Scottish descent. Thomas spoke Welsh as his first language, while Ross spoke Gaelic.

John Ross, on his initial journey to Korea, commencing on May 13, 1873, he visited Korean villages, driven by a deep missionary zeal. Ross traveled along the border between Korea and Manchuria, looking for an opportunity to do mission work with Koreans. He found a Korean village on the upper Amnok River[13] and tried to hire a boat to secretly enter Korea, but no one would help him. At that time, Korea was operating under a policy of isolationism, and anyone who had contact with a foreigner would face execution, so no one was willing to risk renting him a boat. However, Ross befriended a Korean man and gave him several Chinese Bibles.[14]

Continuing to pursue his interest in Korea, he left Yingkou in October 1873. After a week of travel, he arrived at Koryŏ Gate (Korean Gate). While his first visit to Koryŏ Gate was disappointing, it did lead to three important discoveries. First, he confirmed the geographical and strategic importance of Koryŏ Gate. Second, he was able to distribute Chinese Gospels and other books to Koreans. One of the books he brought was a copy of Burns's *The Peep of Day*, which Thomas had used to teach Chinese people in Chefoo.[15] During this visit, Ross found that one of the recipients of this book was

10. Ross, "Visit to the Corean Gate."
11. Shearer, *Wildfire*, 39.
12. Ryang, "First Protestant Missionary to Korea," 73.
13. Kim, "Hankuk Gaesinkyowa Ross Bunyek," 414.
14. Park, *Hanguk Kidok Kyohoe-sa*, 294.
15. Robert Jermain Thomas to LMS, Mar. 15, 1865, Chefoo.

The Martyrdom of Thomas and His Missionary Legacy

a merchant from Uiju, who later gave it to his son, Baek Hong-jun, who would eventually join Ross's translation team. Third, Ross was able to purchase some Korean books.

Between late April and early May 1874, Ross first met Lee Eung-chan. The following year—1875—he returned to the Koryŏ Gate and encountered three young men from Uiju: Baek Heung-Jun, Lee Sung-ha, and Kim Jin-gi. Together they began translating the Bible into Korean. Four years later, all four were baptized by John Macintyre (1837–1905), who served alongside Ross. In 1878, Seo Sang-ryoon and Seong Gyeong-jo met Ross.[16] By late 1881, when Kim Cheong-song sought him out, the translation project had gained new momentum: a community of six Korean believers had formed—and on March 24, 1882, with financial support from the NBSS, the Korean-language Gospel of Luke was translated and published.[17]

By 1887, the full New Testament had been printed. Meanwhile, the Koreans who had taken part in the translation brought printed Bibles into Korea and began distributing them themselves. Ross's Korean translation had been crafted in everyday language that could be understood by common people and women—who together made up some 80 percent of Korea's population—making the Scripture broadly accessible.

> If, therefore, this translation is to the Corean literary man what the Chinese version cannot be, it goes to the women of that country, and to the lowliest and illiterate poor, to speak to them plainly, in language which all understand and employ in daily life, of the wondrous love of Him, who is the Saviour of the world.[18]

The Koreans who had been involved in the translation became colporteurs, bringing the Bibles back into Korea. The very first organized church in Korea, founded by Horace G. Underwood, was Saemunan Presbyterian Church, established in 1887. Of the fourteen Christians who were first baptized there, thirteen had been brought to the faith by Seo Sang-ryoon, who himself had been baptized by John Ross.[19]

> The timing had been actually to sow the seeds; however, we could harvest the first fruits simultaneously. . . . Today, there are two

---

16. Ross, "Corean Version," 37.
17. Ross, "Corean Version," 209.
18. Ross, "Corean Version," 209.
19. Kim, *Hanguk Jonggyo wa Gyohoe Seongjang*, 132.

organized churches in this land with a total membership of over one hundred believers.[20]

The two churches mentioned by Underwood were Saemoonan Church and Sorae Church. Sorae Church was established by Seo Gyeong-jo (1852–1938), the brother of Seo Sang-ryun. Robert Jermain Thomas was the first missionary to enter the Korean interior and preach the gospel. In 1879, thirteen years after Thomas's martyrdom, John Ross, in his book *History of Corea*, recorded the *General Sherman* incident and referred to the "young missionary" Rev. R. J. Thomas.[21] Ross's translation of the Bible into Korean was deeply influenced by Thomas's sacrifice.

Third, Robert Jermain Thomas's death became an invisible landmark in the history of the Korean church. His martyrdom—his faithful endurance unto death—served as a model for succeeding generations of missionaries, and his spirit of self-sacrifice has been treasured and passed down throughout Korean Protestantism.[22] But what, then, is martyrdom?

> The original meaning of the Greek word martyrs was "witness"; in this sense it is often used in the New Testament. Since the most striking witness that Christians could bear to their faith was to die rather than deny it, the word soon began to be used in reference to one who was not only a witness but specifically a witness unto death. This usage is present, at least implicitly, in Acts 22:20 and Revelation 2:13.[23]

Baek Heung-Jun (1848–1893) suffered a great deal during the late Joseon Dynasty. Accused of publishing evil books and organizing illegal assemblies, he was arrested in 1892 for spreading heretical ideas and subjected to torture. When John Ross first visited Goryeo Gate in 1874, he gave a Bible to a Korean merchant from Uiju—the father of Baek Heung-Jun.[24] In 1883, Baek Heung-Jun returned to Korea with several Bibles of his own. In 1892, at the command of Min Byeong-seok, the governor of Pyongyang, Baek Heung-Jun was arrested and imprisoned in Uiju. He was held in prison for two years, subjected to torture and forced to wear the

---

20. Underwood, *Call of Korea*, 136.
21. Ross, *History of Corea*, 94
22. Park, *Hanguk Kidok Kyohoe-sa*, 263.
23. *New Encyclopedia Britannica*, 7:894.
24. Bae, "Three-Self Principle," 132.

"kal" (a heavy wooden collar) until he died in 1893. He is considered the first Protestant Korean martyr.[25]

In 1876, Japan and Korea signed the Ganghwa Island Treaty, and Japanese people began to settle in Korea. They built Shinto shrines to worship the gods of Japan's folk religion. Until 1920, these shrines were built and run by private groups. After that, however, the shrines took on a public and official character under the protection and support of the Japanese government-general of Korea. Japan tried to integrate Japan and Korea by forcing Shintoism on Koreans. Shintoism deified the Japanese emperor and dominated the Japanese spirit, and it was used as a policy of imperialist aggression to support colonial rule.

After the Sino-Japanese War in 1937, the Japanese Government-General of Korea forced all schools and churches to participate in shrine worship. On September 9, 1938, under the watchful eye of the Japanese police, the General Assembly of the Presbyterian Church in Korea voted to approve shrine worship. By June 1945, Japan had built two major shrines and 1,062 smaller shrines in Korea. They also created Shinto altars in all schools and homes and forced people to worship by bowing toward the east every morning. Therefore, opposing shrine worship and the morning bows has a deep meaning in the history of the Korean church. It meant a rejection of idolatry and a commitment to maintaining the purity of the Christian faith. It also holds significant meaning in the history of the Korean people as it represented resistance to Japan's coercion. Many Christian pastors and leaders were executed after suffering harsh oppression and terrible torture during this time.

In 1945, Korea was liberated from Japan. However, the country was soon divided into North and South. In the North, the oppression of Christians began. Christians were exiled to Siberia, coal mines, and concentration camps if they did not renounce their faith. Many Christians were executed. When the Korean War broke out on June 25, 1950, even more Christians were persecuted for their faith under the oppressive communist government.

> At least until 1952 and before the Communist regime oppression, everybody knew about the martyrdom of Reverend Thomas at Daedong River in Pyengyang. His martyrdom was definitely a mental foundation to Christians. . . . The honor and heroic action

---

25. Kim, *Hanguk Gidokgyo Inmulsa*, 50–53.

of Reverend R. J. Thomas were well known to many people together with the tragic situation.[26]

Korean Protestantism counted roughly 250 martyrs before the Korean War. In the final years of the Joseon dynasty, many believers were persecuted on charges of propagating heretical doctrines. Under Japanese colonial rule, those who refused Shinto worship were punished—and during and after the Korean War, nearly one thousand Christians were executed for opposing the materialist revolutionary struggle.[27] Therefore, as Missionary Robert Jermain Thomas was the first Protestant martyr in Korea, it was entirely fitting for Korean Protestantism—with its total of about 1,250 martyrs—to view him as a model of faith and perseverance under persecution.

Fourth, the martyrdom of Thomas ignited a push within the LMS to send missionaries to Korea. Griffith John (1831–1912), originally from South Wales, was the first LMS missionary dispatched to China from Wales, while Thomas followed as the second. Both men had been raised in the same region of Wales, and Thomas's letters show that their families were closely acquainted.[28] When Thomas arrived in Shanghai, he accepted Griffith John's invitation to travel to Korea, and he made three visits to John's mission base in Wuchang.[29]

The first mention of Korea by John can be found in *The Story of Griffith John the Apostle of Central China*, written by Nelson Bitton:

> He volunteered to lead a mission to west China and when there was brought forward a plan for establishing a mission of the LMS in Japan, he volunteered to lead that. He implored the directors of the LMS to begin work in Korea, and it was his deep desire to be allowed to lead a band of missionaries into the hostile province of Hunan.[30]

John's primary concern was for "unreached" regions. Through his travels, he knew about western China and considered Hunan Province one of the most difficult areas to evangelize.[31] He began to see Korea in the

---

26. Rosser, "Korea's First Christian Marty," 16–17.
27. Kim, *Kidokgongbo*, No. 2445, Jun. 12, 2004.
28. Robert Jermain Thomas to parents, Jun. 16, 1866, Peking.
29. Robert Jermain Thomas to LMS, May 15, 1866, Peking.
30. Bitton, *Story of Griffith John*, 75.
31. Thompson, *Griffith John*, 376.

The Martyrdom of Thomas and His Missionary Legacy

same light—as another challenging place to spread the gospel.[32] The news of Thomas's martyrdom reached China in 1867.[33] Just as John had visited Hunan, he deeply respected Thomas for having explored the missionary possibilities in Korea.

Furthermore, in 1868, he urged the directors of the LMS to send missionaries to Korea and establish a mission post there. This is described in *The Life of the Revd Griffith John* written by J. T. Miles in 1900:

> And throughout the years his view of the situation has been that of the pioneer. His horizon has been wide. He reminds the directors of Japan, and wants the Society to be first in the field in Korea.[34]

John's requests to send missionaries to Korea didn't stop there. After hearing the news of the Shino-American Treaty of 1882 on May 22, he repeatedly sent appeals to the LMS on June 1, 6, and 12 of that year, urgently requesting them to dispatch missionaries to Korea:

> I am glad you have started the prayer meetings. That is certainly a step in right direction. Don't forget Korea. Kind regards.[35]

> I want to call the attention of directors to Korea. America has just concluded a treaty with Korea. England will follow immediately. Shall not the LMS be first on the field? *First* or *not* first is a matter of little importance, all I am anxious about is that we should enter in at once. I tried to move the directors to establish a mission in Japan, but in vain. I do trust they will not ignore the claims of Korea.[36]

> The area is estimated at about 80,000 square mile; the population is supposed to be about 10,000,000.[37]

Just one year after Thomas's death in Korea, Griffith John embarked on a five-month missionary journey to western China, a region where no missionaries were present. After returning from his travels, he wrote to the LMS, arguing that they should send missionaries to unreached Korea to preach the Gospel. Unfortunately, the LMS did not act on his request due to

---

32. Bitton, *Story of Griffith John*, 110–11.
33. Alexander Williamson to LMS, Jan. 26, 1867, Chefoo
34. Miles, *Life of Revd Griffith John*, 15.
35. Griffith John to LMS, June 1, 1882, Hankow.
36. Thompson, *Griffith John*, 396–97. John's italics.
37. Griffith John to LMS, June 6, 1822, Hankow.

financial and practical limitations. Nevertheless, John's consistent positive attitude toward Korea from 1868 to 1882 is remarkable.

The books Griffith John wrote were produced at the LMS publishing house in Shanghai and sent to Korea, significantly influencing the country's literature mission.[38] The books that were translated into Korean include *The Gate of Virtue and Wisdom*,[39] *Salient Doctrines of Christianity*,[40] *Truth Concerning God*,[41] *Trimetrical Classic*,[42] and *Leading the Family in the Right Way*.[43]

Up until now, it was widely believed that the first person to ask for missionaries to be sent to Korea was Lee Soo-jung, an attendant to the Korean envoy to Japan. His letter was published in the American missionary journal *The Missionary Review of the World* in March 1884.[44] However, it is now known that Griffith John, influenced by Thomas's martyrdom, made the same appeal to send missionaries to Korea fifteen years earlier.

Fifth, the *General Sherman* incident ultimately paved the way for the Treaty of Amity, Commerce, and Navigation between the United States and Korea—signed in 1882. In 1866, the American government heard about the *General Sherman*'s burning and the death of its crew. The US government began an investigation and considered the possibility of establishing a treaty with Korea. America showed a formal and active interest in Korea by sending two exploratory voyages: one by Robert W. Shufeldt in 1867 and another by John C. Febiger in 1868. On July 31, 1868, Samuel W. Williams, the American acting diplomatic representative in Peking, reported the results of these two voyages to Secretary of State William Henry Seward as follows:

> The whole company on board the General Sherman were killed about September, 1866, and the evidence goes to uphold the presumption that they invoked their sad fate by some rash or violent acts toward the natives.[45]

---

38. Thompson, *Griffith John*, 334–45.
39. Hanguk Gidokgyo Yeoksa Yeonguso, *Hanguk Gidokgyo-ui Yeoksa*, 155.
40. Sungsil Taehakkyo, *Korean Christian Museum*, 259.
41. *Kukmin-ilbo* [People's Daily], Dec. 15, 2005.
42. *Kukmin-ilbo* [People's Daily], Dec. 15, 2005.
43. *Christian Today*, Sept. 23, 2006.
44. Park, *Hanguk Kidok Kyohoe-sa*, 320.
45. Samuel W. Williams to William H. Seward, July 31, 1868; "Mr. Williams to Mr. Seward," *Papers Relating to Foreign Affairs*, 544–45.

The Martyrdom of Thomas and His Missionary Legacy

In the late nineteenth century, opening Korea's ports was one of the biggest issues in American diplomacy. Because of its geopolitical importance as a hub for Eastern trade, the United States—which already had diplomatic ties with Japan and China—could not ignore Korea. In other words, establishing diplomatic relations with Korea was a critical part of America's expansionist policies in Asia.[46]

American historian Charles O. Paullin has commented that

> the most important work of the American navy in the Far East during the third of a century that elapsed between our Civil War and the Spanish-American War was concerned with the Opening of Korea, "the Hermit Nation."[47]

On May 4, 1880, Robert W. Shufeldt (1850–1934), having been granted full authority to establish diplomatic relations with Korea, arrived at the port of Busan. Shufeldt attempted to convey an apology to King Gojong regarding the *General Sherman* incident, but the two never met.[48] He then tried to negotiate a treaty with Korea through Japan, but this effort failed because Japan was against the establishment of diplomatic relations between the US and Korea.[49] Just as Shufeldt was about to give up, he received an invitation from Li Hongzhang (1823–1901), the governor-general of Zhili Province in China.[50]

During this period, Li Hongzhang was in charge of China's foreign affairs and needed America's help to prevent Russia from expanding its influence over both China and Korea. On August 26, 1880, Shufeldt met with Li Hongzhang in Tientsin. This meeting led to the Treaty of Peace, Amity, Commerce, and Navigation between the United States and Korea, which was signed on May 22, 1882, in Jemulpo, Incheon.[51]

As a result of this treaty, churches around the world began to take an interest in missionary work in Korea. Based on Article 11 of the Treaty of Peace, Amity, Commerce, and Navigation, Horace N. Allen was the first American missionary to take up residence in Korea. He initially worked in Shanghai, having been sent by the Presbyterian Church in the USA

---

46. Kim, *Kundae Hanmi Kwangea*, 560.
47. Paullin, *Diplomatic Negotiations*, 282.
48. Paullin, "Opening of Korea," 479.
49. Jones, "Foreign Diplomacy in Korea," 204.
50. Paullin, "Opening of Korea," 481.
51. Lee, *Hanmi Gwangaesa Yeongu*, 164.

(PCUSA) on October 11, 1883.[52] However, he struggled to adapt and, recognizing the need for a missionary in Korea, he received permission from the PCUSA to move there, arriving on September 20, 1884.[53]

Since Korea did not allow missionary work at the time, Allen entered the country as an unpaid doctor at the American legation. He initially served as a physician for foreign diplomats before becoming King Gojong's personal doctor after the Gapsin Coup.

On February 25, 1885, with King Gojong's permission, Allen established Korea's first Western-style hospital, Gwanghyewon.[54] Shortly after, on April 5, 1885, Horace G. Underwood, of the Presbyterian Church, and Henry Appenzeller and his wife, of the Methodist Church, arrived in Jemulpo (Incheon) via Japan.[55] On May 1, 1885, Dr. William Benton Scranton (1856–1922) and his wife arrived, followed by his mother, Mary F. Scranton (1832–1909). In June 1885, a new Presbyterian medical missionary, John H. Heron (1856–90), also entered the country. At this point, the American Methodist and Presbyterian churches were able to establish their mission stations near the American legation in Jeong-dong, Hanyang, and began organized evangelistic work.[56]

The Anglican Church also showed interest in sending missionaries to Korea in the early stages. In late 1885, the Anglican mission in Southern China sent two Chinese missionaries to Busan. On November 1, 1889, Archbishop Benson sent C. J. Corfe (1843–1921) as a missionary to Korea. He arrived on September 29, 1890, with E. B. Landis.[57] J. Henry Davies from the Victorian Presbyterian Church of Australia and his sister, Miss M. T. Davies, arrived in October 1889.[58] The Canadian Presbyterian Church began its missionary work in Korea in 1898.

The *General Sherman* incident did not end with Thomas's death. The event led directly to the Treaty of Peace, Amity, Commerce, and Navigation, which in turn opened the doors for various nations to send missionaries to Korea.

---

52. Ryang, "First Protestant Missionary to Korea," 157.
53. Ryang, "First Protestant Missionary to Korea," 157.
54. Kim, *Hanguk Gyohwasa*, 89–90.
55. Hanguk Gidokgyo Yeoksa Yeonguso, *Hanguk Gidokyo-ui Yeoksa*, 186.
56. Kim, *Hanguk Gyohwasa*, 90.
57. Hanguk Gidokgyo Yeoksa Yeonguso, *Hanguk Gidokyo-ui Yeoksa*, 187.
58. Kim, *Hanguk Gyohwasa*, 90.

The Martyrdom of Thomas and His Missionary Legacy

Sixth, Thomas was not an imperialistic missionary of the nineteenth century, yet he was a casualty of the trade conflicts of the era. It's true that many missionaries in the nineteenth century were influenced by imperialistic thinking. In missionary literature of the time, the three words "commerce," "civilization," and "Christianity" often appeared together as if they were intertwined.[59] I have meticulously analyzed the twenty-one letters Thomas wrote to the LMS from 1856 to 1866 and all the records from the New College board at the University of London. My research shows no indication that Thomas advocated for colonialism. He came to Korea solely out of a missionary conviction that the gospel should be preached to the Korean people:

> Humanly speaking, the Coreans are not at all opposed to the truths of Christianity. The weak hold Indian Buddhism has upon the educated classes in China is still feeble in Corea. I am certain of the fact that our religious books are read with avidity.[60]
>
> The people of Corea, on good testimony, are more accessible to Christian truth than either of the others.[61]

Nevertheless, he was a man of his time. He did seek to go to Korea as an interpreter for a French fleet and conducted his missionary work aboard the *General Sherman*, an armed merchant ship that was there for the purpose of colonial trade. His final letters reveal that Thomas was indeed a missionary living and working in the nineteenth century.

> I have accepted a passage over to Corea, in the schooner of a friendly English merchant.[62]
>
> Little did I think that, last year tempest tossed along a dangerous and inhospitable shore, I should have the honour of being the first Protestant missionary to visit Corea.[63]
>
> Two Roman Catholic Bishops and seven missionaries have been barbarously tortured and then beheaded. For many years these devoted agents of the Papacy have hidden themselves in that almost unknown and strictly watched kingdom.[64]

59. Kane, *Understanding Christian Missions*, 248.
60. Robert Jermain Thomas to LMS, Apr. 4, 1866, Chefoo.
61. Robert Jermain Thomas to LMS, Aug. 1, 1866, Chefoo.
62. Robert Jermain Thomas to LMS, Aug. 1, 1866, Chefoo.
63. Robert Jermain Thomas to LMS, Aug. 1, 1866, Chefoo.
64. Robert Jermain Thomas to LMS, Aug. 1, 1866, Chefoo.

Thomas was not the official interpreter of the *General Sherman*, but because he had some knowledge of the Korean language, he assisted Cho Nung-bong in translation. Despite twice suggesting to Preston and Hogarth that they abandon the mission and return to China, his proposals were rejected. Nevertheless, Thomas cannot be absolved of collective responsibility for the actions of the *General Sherman*.

> The colonial period reached its zenith in the nineteenth century, by which time most of Asia and Africa was parceled out among the European powers. It was that same century which K. S. Latourette called "The Great Century" of modern missions in all parts of the world. Missions and colonialism not only ran a parallel course but they operated in the same regions of the world. It was inevitable, therefore, that these two great forces should meet and mingle.[65]

Therefore, Thomas's entry into Korea aboard the trading vessel *General Sherman* should be studied from a critical perspective by missionaries today. We must reject imperialistic missions that prioritize results over methods. If the goal is righteous, the means to achieve it must also be righteous. History is a study of past events, and our study of the past should inform and help us in the present.

The early Korean church embraced Thomas as a martyr. However, in 1941, as Japan was pushing its "Japan-Korea Unity" policy and launching the Pacific War, they began to criticize Thomas as a vanguard of American imperialist aggression. Today, North Korea continues to teach that Thomas was an American spy who came to occupy Korea.

In the 1980s, the Korean Society of Church History began to focus on Korean church history from the perspective of Korean Christians who embraced Christianity, rather than solely from the records of missionaries. This shift enriched the study of Korean church history. However, Lee Man-yeol, who led this initiative, raised questions about the martyrdom of Thomas. Han Gyoo-moo, agreeing with Lee, clearly states the reasons why he does not consider Thomas a martyr:

> Thomas wanted to do a mission but he miserably died before he could do the mission. However, the important thing is that Koreans did not kill him because he was a missionary. In other words, Thomas did not die because of his mission. . . . If his death was caused by mission, he is a martyr. However, he died because he

---

65. Kane, *Understanding Christian Missions*, 246.

and his ship breached Korean sovereign rights and committed invasive action.⁶⁶

The perspectives on Thomas's death can be understood from several viewpoints.

- First, historical context of early research: In 1928, Oh Mun-hwan published a study on the *General Sherman* incident and Thomas, leading to the publication of *The Life of Reverend Thomas*. For decades, research on Thomas in Korea remained influenced by Oh's narrative. It wasn't until 1970 that Min Kyung-bae introduced a more critical examination of Thomas's role and death.
- Second, challenges in source material: Due to limited and sometimes inaccurate sources, early Korean Protestant narratives often idealized Thomas as the first Protestant martyr in Korea. This romanticized view hindered deeper exploration of his life and mission.
- Third, critiques from historians: Historians like Han Gyoo-moo have questioned the portrayal of Thomas as a martyr, suggesting that such narratives may stem from biased information and Western-centric perspectives. They argue that focusing solely on the negative aspects of Thomas's mission may not provide a balanced historical account.

This debate reflects broader discussions in historiography about the application of positivist methodologies. Leopold von Ranke, a proponent of positivism, emphasized the importance of adhering strictly to verifiable facts in historical writing. While this approach can ensure objectivity, its application to church history is complex. Positivism often excludes divine intervention from historical analysis,⁶⁷ which can be problematic when studying religious history, where such interventions are central to believers' experiences and narratives.

Christian history is the history of missionary endeavors, and the history of missions is the history of missionaries and the Christians who accepted them. Therefore, if one denies the existence and intervention of God in the lives and activities of missionaries, Christian history cannot exist. Thomas began preaching at the age of seventeen and participated in the 1859 Welsh Revival, delivering 156 sermons. His motivation to become a missionary is well documented in his application for missionary candidacy:

---

66. Han, "*General Sherman* Sagunkwa Thomas Sunkyomoonje," 13.
67. Park, *Hanguk Kidok Kyohoe-sa I*, 49–50.

> I have desired to become a missionary for the past five years. The more settled resolve I date from intercourse with various missionaries who passed some evenings with the students of New College. The first motive that influenced me was this. I thought that men of good education, of strong constitution, with ability to acquire languages were wanted for the work and I wished to offer my services more in the spirit of self-denial than anything else. For the last three years I have deliberately after much earnest prayer, resolved to become a missionary, from an earnest longing for Mission work; the downfall of heathenism, the conversion of the heathen. I do most firmly believe that I am appointed by God to be a missionary, and that He has implanted this preference in my heart.[68]

Thomas aspired to become a missionary to preach the pure gospel and convert the heathen. His arrival in Korea was also driven by his desire to conduct mission work based on his faith.

Samuel Moffett, after beginning his mission in Pyongyang in 1893, became aware of Thomas's influence in the city. He also realized that Thomas's death was not a mere incident. In September 1909, at a Korean mission conference of the American Presbyterian Church held in Seoul, he led a resolution to establish the Reverend Thomas Memorial Special Committee. This committee was tasked with collecting materials and information about Thomas.[69]

In 1926, the sixteenth General Assembly of the Presbyterian Church of Korea organized the Thomas Memorial Association for Reverend Thomas's martyrdom. As a result, in 1932, a Thomas Memorial Church was established at a location offering a clear view of the island where Thomas was buried. On September 14, 1932, the dedication service of the Thomas Memorial Church was held. The church's design was in the shape of the letter "T," derived from Thomas's initials.

E. M. Mowry attended the dedication service of the Thomas Memorial Church and wrote the following:

> A beautiful church building was erected last summer on a beautiful site about seven miles below the city of Pyengyang, overlooking the island where Mr. Thomas lies buried. The church is a brick structure with an auditorium 125 feet by 40 feet and a session room, a pastor's study, and a memorial room, which will contain

---

68. Thomas, "Candidate's Answers to the Questions."
69. *Minutes of the Korea Mission*, 1909, 42.

many interesting articles commemorating the life and services of Mr. Thomas ... the church will stand as an expression of the Korean church's appreciation of the zeal and motive that prompted Mr. Thomas visit to Korea.[70]

Critical studies of Robert Jermain Thomas often focus predominantly on the *General Sherman* incident. The *General Sherman* arrived at Joo-Young Port, an inland area of Korea, on August 16, 1866. The period from then until Thomas's martyrdom spanned just seventeen days. Therefore, evaluating Thomas solely through the lens of the *General Sherman* incident is limited and overlooks the broader context of his life and mission. A person's life should be studied comprehensively. For Thomas, the *General Sherman* was merely a "means of transportation" to his mission field. It's essential to distinguish between the *General Sherman* as a transport vessel and Thomas's identity as a missionary.

This work expands upon existing research by incorporating new primary sources related to Robert Jermain Thomas, correcting previously distorted narratives. Particularly, it examines various debates surrounding Thomas's missionary work and the *General Sherman* incident, presenting objective evidence to reassess his life and ministry, which have often been misrepresented in historical accounts.

The central question—whether to view Thomas as a martyr or an aggressor—has been a significant point of contention. Through a thorough analysis of his life and missionary activities, this study finds no evidence suggesting that Thomas harbored intentions to invade Korea, despised the Korean people, or advocated for colonialism. Instead, his life and ministry, characterized by fervent missionary zeal, compel us to interpret his death as martyrdom.

The early Korean Protestant tradition, which regarded Thomas's death as martyrdom, should be preserved. Samuel Moffett's assertion[71] that Korean Christianity began with Thomas's arrival in 1865 resonates profoundly today. Robert Jermain Thomas's status as a martyr and his passionate commitment to missionary work continue to inspire Korean Christians. Despite changes in eras, theology, and historiography, his life, faith, and missionary spirit remain enduring legacies. Studying his beliefs and values is essential for contemporary Christians to inherit and develop this tradition.

70. Mowry, "Dedication," 247–48.
71. Moffett, "Evangelistic Work," 14.

Robert Jermain Thomas's legacy endures through the Bibles he distributed, which continue to be read by many Korean Christians today. His fervent passion for missions has inspired Korean missionaries to be sent abroad to spread the gospel. The following passage from the word of God reflects his legacy:

> For, all men are like grass, and all their glory is like the flowers of the field; the grass withers and the flowers fall, but the word of the Lord stands forever. And this is the word that was preached to you. (1 Peter 1: 24–25)

Melun (Seine et Marne) France,
Rue de Ponthierry 8.
October 26, 1867.

My Dear Sir,

Long before this, I think, you have had a letter from Mr. Edkins, who meant to tell you about my friendly intercourse with your dear regretted son, and who wishes me to write to you all the particulars I recollect of. Here they are.

I met him first in the Summer, 1864, in Peking, at Mr. Edkins', where he was on a visit. I was at once much pleased with the earnestness of his principles, the absence of all cant, joined to the frank and gentlemanly ways which were his own. At that time already, two or three Chinese told me about his being so affable, so pleasing, and how well he spoke their language, which is a very important thing with them. When I knew, some time after, that he had left the Mission, I was sorry for the loss, and asked Mrs. Edkins about the motives. Mr. Thomas being rather independent, said she, sometimes even a little rash or quick, (I am not English, but German, and must beg you to excuse me if I don't always express exactly,) had retired in a discussion, about trifles, with Mr. Muirhead, who might have been more yielding, thought she.

Your son came back to the Mission and to Peking in the Winter 1865–66. At that time, I saw the Edkins once or twice a week, and Mr. Thomas, getting into a kind of intimacy with my son Doctor to the French Legation—I saw a good deal of his ways. They were perfectly evangelical. There was then and I think there is still—in the Chapel joining the London Missionary establishment, a daily and regular preaching from 10-0 in the morning till 4-0 in the afternoon. Between 50 and 100 Chinese, changing now and then, sat listening the Gospel, some patiently, some earnestly, every one decent while coming, sitting or going. Besides these daily evangelical exercises, there was divine service in three different chapels, on Sabbath. All these preachings were afforded by Mr. Edkins, your son and several Chinese catechists. It is a fact that they had more auditors than all the other Missionaries of different Societies five or six together. Few of these numerous listeners accepted the Gospel, but those who did were brought in by the means of your son, as well as by Mr. Edkins and the native catechists.

It frequently happens with us to hear that such a one has been converted by the preaching of such a minister, or the reading of such a book, or the words of such a pious man. Never have I heard of anything of this kind in Peking, though I have been told about many individual conversions. Whenever the first stirring cause mentioned it was the reading of the Scriptures or some christian book. Don't they analyse their feelings as we do? Or are they more influenced by the truth itself written in tolerable Chinese than by the most eloquent preacher, who, I dare say, is but a poor Chinese scholar to their fastidious ears. I mention this in answer to Mr. Edkins' question, whether I recollect of any instance of particular usefulness to tell you about your son. Were I asked the same question about Mr. Edkins, I couldn't quote one case where a Chinese confessed that his heart had been awakened by him, and yet many of them have frequently told me, in a general way, that he is a good man. Nothing more. While as I feel and say with enthusiasm that he is the best man I ever knew. And then he has been the means, and he alone, of the first conversions, he formed and instructed and does so still the native catechists, he established the first christian school in Peking, he keeps the work up, quiet, faithful, amidst great difficulties. But your son, too has been very useful, there is no doubt. And in course of time, he would have been so more and more because of some particular qualities to win the Chinese. They are very particular in many things.

The lowest peasant in the fields is not always willing to answer a stranger's question about the road or so, if it is not preceded by asking the man's "honourable home," his "precious age," and so forth. Every Missionary knows these rules of Chinese etiquette, but few will mind them. Your son did. On the other hand, they expect in a gentleman that kind of dignified quietness which is the stamp of education in Europe. Your son was in full possession of these qualities; he told me that he studied them, as most important, in Mr. Edkins. And they were natural to him. His extraordinary talent for languages showed a quick observation of other people's ways, and the facility to make them his own. In two instances, Mr. Thomas' tact quite astonished my son. He was now and then taking photographies, as amateur. Your son proposed him the portrait of Foah-Sheng (Buddha living). This man is looked at by the lower classes as an incarnation of Buddha. Some high Mandarins, in a friendly conversation with one of our French interpreters, compared him to the Pope, with the difference, said they, that the Pope is elected by the priests, and independent, while our Government chooses the child to be Foah-Sheng, after the death of the present, which makes him dependent. At any rate, Foah-Sheng is a high official, almost a deity, and as much as I know, there are no strangers in Peking who come near him, except once, some Roman Catholic

Missionaries, together with the gentlemen of the French Legation, during and after a Buddha Ceremony. How Mr. Thomas had found his way to him, I don't know; but he had, introduced my son, who took the man's photograph, and was highly pleased by the friendly tone of Mr. Thomas' intercourse with Foah-Sheng. Another day, Mr. Thomas proposed my son, also for photographies, to take him to the temple of heaven, the entrance of which was, at that time, forbidden to strangers. They got easily in, but soon after, they were disturbed by some Mandarins of that kind which can't be bought by some Dollars. They were in a perfect wrath. Well, Mr. Thomas talked so much and so well, he was so polite and so dignified, that he quite soothed the Chinese gentlemen, and parted with them in the most friendly way.

This knowledge of Chinese language and etiquette might have given him, by and by, an opening in high society which no Missionary in Peking at least, has been trying yet. As it were, it became the cause of the last deciding event of his life.

Nine Roman Catholic Missionaries had been murdered in Corea. M. de Bellonet, French Charge d'affaires in Peking, was immediately determined to punish the offence, and invited Admiral Rose, then at Chefoo, to sail without delay. One missionary only had escaped, besides him there was no interpreter. M. Lemaine, first interpreter to the French Legation, suggested your son as one who might be highly useful. He had been in Corea, knew the language, and was fitted for the affair because of those qualities just now mentioned, and which his Peking friends so well knew and appreciated in him. The Missionaries in Peking, of five different boards, have established a rule according to which they decide, by vote or persuasion, every important question. In this occurrence, Mr. Edkins told me, there were two against. One, an American, by political antipathy, (this was my idea, not Mr. Edkins', it was at the time of the Mexicans bitterness,) the other, Mr. Edkins said, because it was for a Roman Catholic interest. There I gave a start. "Do you prefer Buddhists to Roman Catholics, and won't you ally with them who are so cruelly offended? Unless you are against any kind of war." "That is my own view," replied Mr. Edkins, "we have another meeting to-night, and I think we'll bring the two opponents round." So they did, with difficulty or without, I don't know. Most probably they considered a Missionary interest besides the humane one, to assist their christian brethren, the Roman Catholics.

The Coreans are tributaries to the Chinese Government, and a great number of them are staying every Winter in Peking.

Individually they seem good-natured, confident, and more disposed to familiarity with strangers than the Chinese those who read Chinese are glad to accept christian books. Your son had been sent, in 1865, to Corea for the study of the language, had he not? So the Peking Missionaries thought perhaps that another stay in Corea might give him some advantage for the opening of the Gospel, but, I repeat it, this is my own supposition, I never was told nor inquired about the final meeting for the subject. I know by M. Lemaine, our French interpreter, that M. de Bellonet was very happy to secure Mr. Thomas, and that he wished to settle immediately the pecuniary appointment. Mr. Thomas objected that this was the Missionary establishment's business, not his; he also refused any advance of money for the voyage expenses. Mr. Edkins joined a young native, skilled in map drawing. Some days after their departure from Peking, we too left and met your son at Cien-Chin, waiting for sailing conveniently. A week after, the French Consul of that place communicated to your son a letter from M. de Bellonet, who informed him that there was no more occasion for Mr. Thomas' going to Chefon in order to join Admiral Rose, who had left for Saigon. Mr. Thomas thought these news inexact, so did we. "I have an idea" said he, "to go at any rate to Chefoo. There is a man who owes me some money which I'll never have without going myself, and which is more than the voyage expenses. What do you think?" We joined his views. My son, being persuaded that the expedition would take place, calculated how much Mr. Thomas' individuality would suit the Admiral whom he had known in Peking. I didn't think of that, but I recollect some words of Dr. Mullens, who said in Mr. Edkins' parlour in Peking, September or October, 1865—that Missionaries are some times too apt to think themselves necessary for the mark they are at, that they hesitate too often to take a change when they really want it, and that when they have had it, they come back so much more capable and valuable. I knew that Mr. Edkins always finds means for the work he has at hand, and in this case, he had settled things for a long absence of Mr. Thomas. Let the young man follow his natural desire for moving, thought I. So he went.

Some days after, we too sailed for Chefoo, on our way home. Mr. Thomas had kindly secured a house and boarding for our party, my son, my daughter-in-law, and two grandchildren, besides myself; he came on board the Steamer and took us down. Then he told us what we thought at Cien-Chin; Admiral Rose was expected back, and had left orders for the expedition. A fortnight after this, your son called and told me that he was going to Corea without waiting for Admiral Rose, who was certain to come, (he came indeed a fortnight after, and has been to Corea,) and would be glad to find his way prepared by such enquiries as Mr. Thomas could get. "You'll excuse me if I don't tell you by what ship I am sailing." This was said very politely, but in that decided tone which admits no gainsaying. Alas! I never saw him again. Many months after, I read here, in a French paper, the frightful news. I was very sick at the time, and had the most melancholy leisure to fancy and picture out the probable scenes of the cruel event. Nor did I shrink from it. Bitter has been his pang, but short we may think, and Jesus was by to comfort him in this dark valley of death, that we must hope. His promises are Amen. As far as human eye can see, your son did love the Lord, he did serve him so we may be sure that he has reached a blessed home, whilst we are still striving against and suffering from sin. Thy will be done! Our bitter and though happy day will come too, at last.

One word more. We were told at Shanghai, three weeks or more after the sailing of the "General Sherman," that she was a smuggler. I think this is true, because Mr. Thomas didn't wish to tell me what ship he was sailing by he felt that I would have been against. But, I am sorry to say, smuggling is so general in China that it is little thought of. I asked a Shanghai merchant "To be sure, you don't smuggle?" "Indeed I do, every one does." He blushed though. I knew it is so. Even christian people are influenced by the bad moral atmosphere they are breathing in. The well-known Chinese Missionary, Gutzlaff, has been taking advantage, in his time, of opium vessels. He sailed by, and when the Captain and crew went on shore for their business, he did his, namely, distributing the Scripture and preaching the Gospel. I saw this fact in "The Middle Kingdom," By Dr. Wells T. Williams, formerly a Missionary at Canton, now Secretary to the United States Legation in Peking. Had it pleased the Lord to spare your son's life, and give him success in spreading the Gospel in Corea, twenty years hence no-one would enquire how he went there, but his name would be glorified as Gutzlaff's is now. Happy we are that men don't judge us, but the Lord, or rather that the blood of Christ washes away our sins, and your son's mistakes too. Those who have known him will always keep a kind and interesting souvenir.

Please, my dear Sir, to accept my deep felt sympathy, and let me hope that my letter has brought a slight comfort to your wounded heart.

PAULINE MORACHE

Bibliography

Adroddiad Jubili Dyled Siloh, Glandŵr, Abertawe, 1900. Yn cynnwys Amlinelliad o Hanes yr Eglwys yn y lle, yn nghyd ag Enwau y tanysgrifwyr at y Jubili [Report of the debt Jubilee of Siloh, Glandŵr, Swansea, 1900, including an outline of the history of the church in that place together with the names of subscribers to the Jubilee]. Swansea, KR: Siloh Church, 1901.

Allen, Roland. *Missionary Methods: St. Paul's or Ours?* Grand Rapids: Eerdmans, 1962.

Bae, An-ho. "The Three-Self Principle and the Mission Method of John Ross: A Study on the Formation of the Early Korean Presbyterian Church (1874–1893)." PhD diss., King's College, University of Aberdeen, 2001.

Baek, Nak-Jun. *Han'guk Gaesin Kyohoe-sa 1832–1910* [The history of Protestant missions in Korea 1832–1910]. Seoul: Yessei University Press, 1973.

Bethlehem Church. "Bethlehem Eglwys yr Annibynwyr, Rhosllannerchrugog. Adroddiad Blynyddol" [Annual report of Bethlehem Independent Church, Rhosllannerchrugog]. 2009.

Bird, Isabella Lucy. *The Yangtze Valley and Beyond.* Cambridge: Cambridge University Press, 1899.

Bishop, I. B. *The Yangtze Valley and Beyond.* Cambridge: Cambridge University Press, 1899.

Bitton, Nelson. *The Story of Griffith John: The Apostle of Central China.* Edinburgh: Morrison & Gibb, 1928.

Cavendish, Alfred Edward John. *Korea and the Sacred White Mountain: Being a Brief Account of a Journey in Korea in 1891.* London: George Philip & Son, 1894.

China Mission Handbook. Shanghai: American Presbyterian Mission Press, 1896. https://archive.org/details/chinamissionhandoounse_1.

Congregational Year Book. London: Congregational Union of England and Wales, 1859, 1864, 1866, 1868, 1879.

Dallet, Charles. *Histoire de l'Eglise en Coree* [History of the Korean Catholic]. 2 vols. Paris: Victor Palme, 1874.

Davis, George Thompson Brown. *Korea for Christ.* New York: Fleming H. Revell, 1910.

Dongbuk-a Yeoksa Jaedan [Northeast Asian History Foundation]. *Manju Geu Ttang, Saram Geurigo Yeoksa* [Manchuria: The land, people, and history]. Seoul: Dongbuk-a Yeoksa Jaedan, 2007.

Evans, Eifion. *Revival Comes to Wales.* Bridgend, UK: Bryntirion, 1995.

Bibliography

Foreign Mission Board of the United Free Church of Scotland. "Meeting Minutes No. 3446." 1883–1884. Available at School of Oriental and African Studies (SOAS) Archives, University of London.

Gale, J. S. "The Fate of the General Sherman: From an Eye Witness." *The Korean Repository* 2 (1895) 252–54.

General Council of Protestant Evangelical Missions in Korea. *The Korea Mission Field*. Dec. 1932.

Gibbard, Noel. *Griffith John: Apostle to China*. Bridgend, UK: Bryntirion, 1998.

Gill, David W. *Christian Missions to China in the 19th Century*. Cambridge: Cambridge University Press, 2002.

Goh, Moo-song. *Thomaswa hamgea denanun soonrea yeohaeng* [Make a Pilgrimage with Thomas]. Seoul: Qumran, 2004.

———. "Western and Asian Portrayals of Robert Jermain Thomas (1839–1866), Pioneer Protestant Missionary to Korea: A Historical Study of an East-West Encounter Through His Mission." PhD diss., University of Birmingham, 1995.

Gojong Taehwangje Sillok [Annals of King Gojong]. Vol. 48, 1865–1868. Seoul: Kuksa Pyenchan Wewonhoi, 1970.

Green, Michael J. *Robert Jermain Thomas: Martyr and Missionary*. Cambridge: Cambridge University Press, 1995.

Griffis, Elliot William. *Corea, the Hermit Nation*. New York: Charles Scribners' Sons, 1902.

Griffith, G. Penar. *Hanes Bywgraffiadol o Genadon Cymreig i Wledydd Paganaidd, yn nghyd a rhestr o'r rhai sydd eto yn fyw* [Biographical histories of Welsh missionaries to pagan lands, along with a list of those still alive]. Caerdydd, UK: Gwaith Argraffu Deheudir Cymru, 1897.

Guksapyeonchan Wiwonhoe. *Geosang, Jeonguk Sanggwon-eul Jangakhada* [Great merchants: Seizing the national market, Korean culture history III]. Seoul: Doosan Donga, 2005.

Hall, Basil. *Voyage to Loo-Choo, and Other Places in the Eastern Seas, in the Year 1816*. Edinburgh: James Ballantyne, 1826.

Hall, Sherwood. *With a Stethoscope in Asia: Korea*. McLean, VA: MLC Associates, 1978.

Han, Kyu-moo. "General Sherman Sagunkwa Thomas Sunkyomoonje" [The General Sherman incident]. *Hankuk Kidokkyo Yëk-sa* [Korean Christianity and History] 8 (1998).

Hanguk Gidokgyo Yeoksa Yeonguso [Institute for Korean Christian History]. *Hanguk Gidokgyo-ui Yeoksa* [History of Korean Christianity]. Vol. 1. Seoul: Christian Literature Mission, n.d.

Hattaway, Paul. *China's Book of Martyrs: AD 845–Present*. The Fire and Blood Series 1. Carlisle, UK: Piquant, 2007.

Heyl, Eric. "Early American Steamers." Vol. 1. https://babel.hathitrust.org/cgi/pt?id=mdp.39015024193131&seq=364.

Hiebert, Paul G. *Anthropological Insights for Missionaries*. Ada, MI: Baker, 1985.

Jay, William. *Morning Exercises for the Closet*. London: Hamilton, Adams, 1835.

Jones, F. C. "Foreign Diplomacy in Korea 1866–1894." MA diss., Harvard University, 1935.

Jones, R. Brinley. *Floreat Landubriense: Celebrating a Century and a Half of Education at Llandovery College*. Llandovery, UK: Trustees of Llandovery College, 1998.

Jones, T. Gwyn, and Joseph Jones. *Brecon and Radnor Congregationalism 1662*. Commemoration ed. Merthyr Tydfil, UK: Joseph Williams & Son, 1912.

Kane, J. H. *Understanding Christian Missions*. Ada, MI: Baker, 1978.

BIBLIOGRAPHY

Kim, Hak-kwan. *Jungkuk Kyohoe-sa* [History of the Chinese church]. Seoul: Irehsewon, 2005.
Kim, Ji-hyun. *Seontaekbadeun Seom Baengnyeongdo* [The Chosen Island Baengnyeongdo]. Seoul: Abel Seowon, 2002.
Kim, Kwang-su. *Hanguk Gidokgyo Inmulsa* [History of Korean Christian Figures]. Seoul: Hanguk Gidokgyosa Yeonguso, 1981.
Kim, Myoung-ho. *Chogi Hanmi Gwangyeui Jaejomyeong* [A reexamination of early Korea–US Relations]. Seoul: Yeoksa Bipyeongsa, 2005.
———. *Hwanjae Pak Kyu-Su* [A Study on Hwanjae Pak Kyu-Su]. Seoul: Changbi, 2008.
Kim, Seong-tea. "General Sherman Sagune Deahan Hankuk Jungbu-Kirok" [R. J. Thomas and the General Sherman Incident]. *Bokum ka Sangwhang* [Gospel and Circumstances] 7 (1995) 132–38.
Kim, Su-jin. *Jungguk Gaesingyosa* [History of Chinese Protestantism]. Seoul: Hongseongsa, 1997.
Kim, Sung-tae. *Seongyo wa Munhwa* [Mission and Culture]. Seoul: Ire Seowon, 2000.
Kim, Sun-guen. *Kidokgongbo* [Christian newspaper]. June 12, 2004.
Kim, Won-mo. *Kundae Hanmi Kwangea-sa* [A Modern History of United States and Korean Relationship]. Seoul: Cheolhakgwa Hyeonsil, 1992.
Kim, Yang-sun. *Hanguk Gyohisa Yeongu*. Seoul: Kidokgyo Mun-sa, 1971.
———. "Hankuk Gaesinkyowa Ross Bunyek" [Ross Version and Korean Protestantism]. *Beaksan Hakbo* [Beaksan: A school bulletin]. Vol. 3. Seoul: Beaksan Hakhoi, 1967.
Kim, Yeon-taek. *Hanguk Jonggyo wa Gyohoe Seongjang* [Korean Religion and Church Growth]. Anyang, KR: Daehan Theological Seminary Press, 1998.
Kim, Young-jae. *Hanguk Gyohwasa* [Korean Church History]. Suwon, KR: Hapdong Theological Seminary Press, 2004.
Kwahak Paekkwa Chulpan-sa [Institute of Historical Research, Academy of Social Sciences]. *Chosön Chönsa* [A Comprehensive History of Korea]. Vol. 13. Pyongyang, KP: Science & Encyclopedia, 1980.
Latourette, Kenneth Scott. *The Great Century: North Africa and Asia*. A History of the Expansion of Christianity 6. London: Harper & Brothers, 1944.
———. *A History of Christianity*. New York: Harper & Brothers, 1953.
———. *A History of Protestant Missions in China*. London: Society for Promoting Christian Knowledge, 1929.
Lee, Duk-ju. *Naraui Dokrip, Kyohoiui Dokrip* [Independence of Nation and Church]. Seoul: Kidokkyomun-sa, 1991.
Lee, Jin-ho. *Dongyang-ül Sömgin Kwichüllapü* [Karl Gützlaff: A missionary who served the Orient]. Seoul: Amen, 1998.
Lee, Man-yeol. *Hanguk Kidokgyosa Teukgang* [Special topics in Korean church history]. Seoul: ESP, 1999.
Lee, Min-sik. *Hanmi Gwangaesa Yeongu* [A Study on the History of Korea-US Relations]. Seoul: Jeonhun, 1996.
London Missionary Society. "Annual Report of the LMS for 1867." Available at School of Oriental and African Studies (SOAS) Archives, University of London.
———. "Arrival of Missionaries in China: Letter from Rev. William Muirhead." *The Missionary Magazine and Missionary Chronicle* 334.51, Mar. 1, 1864. https://archive.org/details/missionarymagazi3345lond/page/56/mode/2up.

Bibliography

———. "Death of Mrs. Thomas, of Shanghae, China." *The Missionary Magazine and Chronicle* 338.55, July 1, 1863. https://archive.org/details/missionarymagazi3385lond/page/220/mode/2up.

———. "Departure of Missionaries for China." *The Missionary Magazine and Chronicle* 327.44, Aug. 1, 1863. https://archive.org/details/missionarymagazi3274lond/page/250/mode/2up.

———. "Minutes of Eastern Committee, China." 1865.

———. "Record of the Reverend R. Jermain Thomas." LMS Archives. Available at School of Oriental and African Studies (SOAS) Archives, University of London.

———. "Visit of the R. J. Thomas to Corea." *The Missionary Magazine and Chronicle* 362.79, July 2, 1866. https://archive.org/details/missionarymagazi3627lond/page/200/mode/2up.

Maclay, Edgar Stanton. *A History of the United States Navy, 1775–1901*. New York: D. Appleton, 1901.

McCune, G. M., and J. A. Harrison, eds. *Korean-American Relations Documents Pertaining to the Far Eastern Diplomacy of the United States: The Initial Period, 1883–1886*. Vol. 1. Berkeley: University of California Press, 1951.

Miles, J. T. *The Life of the Revd Griffith John*. London: LMS, 1908.

Min, Gyeong-bae. *Kyohoe-wa Minjok* [Church and People]. Seoul: Korean Christian, 1981.

Moffett, Samuel A. "Evangelistic Work." Quarto-Centennial Conference Paper read at the Korea Mission of the PCUSA at the annual meeting in Pyen Yang. Aug. 27, 1909.

———. *A History of Christianity in Asia*. Vol. II. New York: Orbis, 2005.

Mowry, E. M. "Dedication of the Thomas Memorial Church." *Korea Mission Field* 28.12 (1932) 247–48.

"Mr. Williams to Mr. Seward." *Papers Relating to Foreign Affairs, Accompanying the Annual Message of the President, to the Third Session Fortieth Congress*. Part 1. Washington, DC: Government Printing Office, 1869. https://babel.hathitrust.org/cgi/pt?id=mdp.39015050719668&seq=7.

Munemitsu, Mutsu. *Geonjeong-rok*. Seoul: Bumwoo-sa, 1993.

National Bible Society of Scotland. "NBSS Annual Report for 1865." Available at School of Oriental and African Studies (SOAS) Archives, University of London.

———. "NBSS Annual Report for 1866." Available at School of Oriental and African Studies (SOAS) Archives, University of London.

Neill, Stephen. *A History of Christian Missions*. London: Penguin, 1990.

New College Divinity School. "The Minutes of Council." Edinburgh, UK: University of Edinburgh, 1853–1856.

New Encyclopaedia Britannica. Chicago: Encyclopædia Britannica, 1994.

Nuttall, G. F. *New College, London and Its Library*. London: Dr. Williams' Trust, 1977.

Oak, Sung-Deuk. "1866 Pyeongyangyangnan kwa Thomas ui Sunkyo, Geu Haeseoksa" [Interpreting the 1866 Pyongyang Disturbance and the Martyrdom of Robert Jermain Thomas']. *Gidokgyosasang* [Korean Christianity] 721 (2019) 187–200.

———. *The Making of Korean Christianity: Protestant Encounters with Korean Religions, 1876–1915*. Waco, TX: Baylor University Press, 2013.

Oh, Mun-hwan. *Kidokgongbo* [Christian newspaper]. Jan. 15, 1957.

———. *Kidok Sinbo* [Christian News]. Jan. 15, 1957.

———. *Thomas Moksa-jeon* [The Life of R. J. Thomas who was killed at Pyongyang in 1866]. Pyongyang, KP: TMA, 1928.

Bibliography

———. *Thomas moksa soonkyo gineam geundohoy saryo* [Twenty-five years of the TMA]. Seoul: TMA, 1947.
———. "The Two Visits of the Rev. R. J. Thomas to Korea." *Transactions of the Korea Branch of the Royal Asiatic* 19 (1930) 93–123.
Owen, John. *The Death of Death in the Death of Christ*. London: Banner of Truth, 1959.
Oxford Dictionary of National Biography. Oxford: Oxford University Press, 2004.
Pak, Kyu-su. *Cheonjip* [Complete Collection of Pak Kyu-su]. 2 vols. Seoul: Asea Munhwa-sa, 1978.
———. *Jang-kea* [Official Memorials]. 1866.
Park, Yong-gyu. *Hanguk Kidok Kyohoe-sa I* [Korean church history]. Seoul: Word of Life, 2004.
———. "Robert J. Thomas Seongyosa: Yeoksajeok Pyeongga" [Robert J. Thomas, Missionary: Historical Evaluation]. In *Thomas Seongyosa Sun-gyo 150ju-nyeon Ginyom Simpozium* [The 150th anniversary symposium of the martyrdom of Missionary Thomas], 1–60. Seoul: Hanguk Gidokgyo-sa Yeonguso, 2016.
Paullin, Charles Oscar. *Diplomatic Negotiations of American Naval Officers 1778–1883*. Baltimore, MD: Johns Hopkins University Press, 1912.
———. "The Opening of Korea by Commodore Shufeldt." *Political Science Quarterly* 25 (1910) 470–99.
Rees, Thomas, and John Thomas. *Hanes Eglwysi Annibynnol Cymru*, Cyf. I [A history of the Welsh Independent Churches, Vol. 1]. Liverpool, UK: Swyddfa "Y Tyst Cymreig," 1871.
Rhodes, Harry A. *History of the Korea Mission, Presbyterian Church, USA, 1884–1934*. Seoul: Choson Mission Presbyterian Church USA, 1938.
"Robert Thomas Retirement Address." *Abergavenny Chronicle and Monmouthshire Advertiser*, Feb. 15, 1884.
Ross, John. "Corean Version of the New Testament." The Missionary Record of the United Presbyterian Church, Feb. 1881.
———. "Visit to the Corean Gate." *Chinese Record and Missionary Journal* (Nov./Dec. 1875) 349–54.
Rosser, E. M. "Korea's First Christian Martyr." *The Evangelical Magazine of Wales* 16.3 (1977) 16–17.
Ryang, J. S. "The First Protestant Missionary to Korea." *Korea Mission Field* 30.7 (1934) 154–55.
Seonggyochwalli [Salient Doctrines of Christianity]. https://library.yonsei.ac.kr/search/detail/CAT000000084101?briefLink=/main/searchBrief?q=%EC%84%B1%EA%B5%90%EC%B4%AC%EB%A6%AC.
Shearer, Roy E. *History of Corea, Ancient and Modern with Description of Manners and Customs, Language and Geography*. Paisley, UK: J. and R. Parlane, 1879.
———. *Wildfire: Church Growth in Korea*. Grand Rapids: Eerdmans, 1966.
Shufeldt, Robert W. "Corea's Troubles." *San Francisco Chronicle*, Oct. 30, 1887.
Sibree, J. "LMS Register of Missionaries and Deputations (1923)." *Dictionary of Welsh Biography*. London Missionary Society Records.
Silverstone, Paul. H. *Warships of the Civil War Navies*. Annapolis, MD: Naval Institute, 1989.
Somerville, W. C. *From Iona to Dunblane: The Story of the NBSS to 1948*. Edinburgh: McLagan and Cumming, 1948.

Bibliography

Steer, Roger. *J. Hudson Taylor: A Man in Christ*. Missionary Life Stories. Milton Keynes, UK: OMF, 1990.

Sungsil Taehakkyo [Soongsil University]. *The Korean Christian Museum at Soongsil University*. Seoul: Tongchen, 2004.

Thomas, George F. *Congregationalists and the Church in the Nineteenth Century*. Oxford: Oxford University Press, 1980.

Thomas, John. *Hanes Eglwysi Annibynnol Cymru*. Cyf. V [A history of the Welsh Independent Churches. Vol. 5]. Dolgellau, UK: Swyddfa 'Y Tyst Cymreig', 1891.

Thomas, Robert Jermain. "The Candidate's Answers to the Questions." London Missionary Society Records. July 22, 1862.

Thompson, R. Wardlaw. *Griffith John: The Story of Fifty Years in China*. London: Religious Tract Society, 1906.

Underwood, H. G. *Call of Korea*. New York: Fleming H. Revell, 1908.

Williamson, Alexander. *Journeys in North China, Manchuria, and Eastern Mongolia; with Some Account of Corea*. Vol. 2. London: Smith, Elder, 1870.

Woo, Kyung-sup. "Joseon Junghwajueui-e daehan Hakseolsajeok Geomto" [A theoretical study on the Confucian Universalism in the late Joseon Dynasty]. *Hanguksa Yeongu* 159 (2012) 237–63.

www.ingramcontent.com/pod-product-compliance
Lightning Source LLC
Chambersburg PA
CBHW072143160426
43197CB00012B/2228